POST-SYNODAL APOSTOLIC EXHORTATION

*CHRISTUS VIVIT*

OF THE HOLY FATHER

FRANCIS

TO YOUNG PEOPLE

AND TO THE ENTIRE PEOPLE OF GOD

LIBRERIA EDITRICE VATICANA | United States Conference of Catholic Bishops

Copyright © 2019, Libreria Editrice Vaticana (LEV),
Vatican City State. All rights reserved.

Photo: CNS/Paul Haring

Publication No. 7-628

United States Conference of Catholic Bishops
Washington, DC

ISBN 978-1-60137-628-2

Published in the United States, April 2019
First printing, April 2019

# Contents

CHAPTER ONE:
WHAT DOES THE WORD OF GOD
HAVE TO SAY ABOUT YOUNG PEOPLE? . . . . . . . .2
In the Old Testament . . . . . . . . . . . . . . . . . . . . . . . . . . . .2
In the New Testament . . . . . . . . . . . . . . . . . . . . . . . . . . .3

CHAPTER TWO:
JESUS, EVER YOUNG . . . . . . . . . . . . . . . . . . . . . . . . .7
Jesus' Youth . . . . . . . . . . . . . . . . . . . . . . . . . . . . . . . . . . .7
His Youth Teaches Us . . . . . . . . . . . . . . . . . . . . . . . . . . .10
The Youth of the Church . . . . . . . . . . . . . . . . . . . . . . . . .11
        A Church Open to Renewal . . . . . . . . . . . . . . 12
        A Church Attentive to the Signs of the Times . . . 13
Mary, the Young Woman of Nazareth . . . . . . . . . . . . . . . .15
Young Saints . . . . . . . . . . . . . . . . . . . . . . . . . . . . . . . . . .17

CHAPTER THREE:
YOU ARE THE "NOW" OF GOD . . . . . . . . . . . . . . .20
In Positive Terms . . . . . . . . . . . . . . . . . . . . . . . . . . . . . . .20
Many Ways of Being Young. . . . . . . . . . . . . . . . . . . . . . .21
Some Experiences of Young People. . . . . . . . . . . . . . . . . .22
        Living in a World in Crisis . . . . . . . . . . . . . . 22
        Desires, Hurts and Longings . . . . . . . . . . . . 25
The Digital Environment . . . . . . . . . . . . . . . . . . . . . . . . .27
Migrants as an Epitome of Our Time . . . . . . . . . . . . . . . .29
Ending Every Form of Abuse. . . . . . . . . . . . . . . . . . . . . .31
A Way Out. . . . . . . . . . . . . . . . . . . . . . . . . . . . . . . . . . . .35

CHAPTER FOUR:
A GREAT MESSAGE FOR ALL
YOUNG PEOPLE. . . . . . . . . . . . . . . . . . . . . . . . . . . . .38
A God Who Is Love . . . . . . . . . . . . . . . . . . . . . . . . . . . .38
Christ Saves You . . . . . . . . . . . . . . . . . . . . . . . . . . . . . . .40

He Is Alive! . . . . . . . . . . . . . . . . . . . . . . . . . . . . . . . . . .42
The Spirit Gives Life . . . . . . . . . . . . . . . . . . . . . . . . . . . .44

CHAPTER FIVE:
PATHS OF YOUTH . . . . . . . . . . . . . . . . . . . . . . . . . . .46
A Time of Dreams and Decisions . . . . . . . . . . . . . . . . . . .46
A Thirst for Life and Experience. . . . . . . . . . . . . . . . . . . .49
In Friendship with Christ . . . . . . . . . . . . . . . . . . . . . . . . .51
Growth in Maturity . . . . . . . . . . . . . . . . . . . . . . . . . . . . .54
Paths of Fraternity . . . . . . . . . . . . . . . . . . . . . . . . . . . . . .56
Young and Committed . . . . . . . . . . . . . . . . . . . . . . . . . . .58
Courageous Missionaries . . . . . . . . . . . . . . . . . . . . . . . . . .60

CHAPTER SIX:
YOUNG PEOPLE WITH ROOTS . . . . . . . . . . . . . . .63
Don't Allow Yourselves to Be Uprooted . . . . . . . . . . . . . .63
Your Relationship with the Elderly . . . . . . . . . . . . . . . . . .65
Dreams and Visions . . . . . . . . . . . . . . . . . . . . . . . . . . . . .67
Taking Risks Together . . . . . . . . . . . . . . . . . . . . . . . . . . .69

CHAPTER SEVEN:
YOUTH MINISTRY . . . . . . . . . . . . . . . . . . . . . . . . . . .71
A Pastoral Care That Is Synodal . . . . . . . . . . . . . . . . . . . .71
Main Courses of Action. . . . . . . . . . . . . . . . . . . . . . . . . . .73
Suitable Environments . . . . . . . . . . . . . . . . . . . . . . . . . . .75
        Youth Ministry in Educational Institutions . . . . . 77
Areas Needing to Be Developed . . . . . . . . . . . . . . . . . . . .79
A "Popular" Youth Ministry . . . . . . . . . . . . . . . . . . . . . . .82
Always Missionaries. . . . . . . . . . . . . . . . . . . . . . . . . . . . . .85
Accompaniment by Adults . . . . . . . . . . . . . . . . . . . . . . . .86

CHAPTER EIGHT:
VOCATION . . . . . . . . . . . . . . . . . . . . . . . . . . . . . . . . . .89
God's Call to Friendship . . . . . . . . . . . . . . . . . . . . . . . . . .89
Being There for Others . . . . . . . . . . . . . . . . . . . . . . . . . . .90
Love and Family . . . . . . . . . . . . . . . . . . . . . . . . . . . . . . .92

Work . . . . . . . . . . . . . . . . . . . . . . . . . . . . . . . . . . . . . . . .95
The Vocation to Special Consecration . . . . . . . . . . . . . . . . .97

**CHAPTER NINE:**
**DISCERNMENT** . . . . . . . . . . . . . . . . . . . . . . . . . . . . . . . . .99
Discerning Your Vocation . . . . . . . . . . . . . . . . . . . . . . . . . .100
The Call of Jesus Our Friend . . . . . . . . . . . . . . . . . . . . . .102
Listening and Accompaniment . . . . . . . . . . . . . . . . . . . . .103
And to Conclude . . . a Wish. . . . . . . . . . . . . . . . . . . . . . . .106

1. CHRIST IS ALIVE! He is our hope, and in a wonderful way he brings youth to our world, and everything he touches becomes young, new, full of life. The very first words, then, that I would like to say to every young Christian are these: Christ is alive and he wants you to be alive!

2. He is in you, he is with you and he never abandons you. However far you may wander, he is always there, the Risen One. He calls you and he waits for you to return to him and start over again. When you feel you are growing old out of sorrow, resentment or fear, doubt or failure, he will always be there to restore your strength and your hope.

3. With great affection, I address this Apostolic Exhortation to all Christian young people. It is meant to remind you of certain convictions born of our faith, and at the same time to encourage you to grow in holiness and in commitment to your personal vocation. But since it is also part of a synodal process, I am also addressing this message to the entire People of God, pastors and faithful alike, since all of us are challenged and urged to reflect both on the young and for the young. Consequently, I will speak to young people directly in some places, while in others I will propose some more general considerations for the Church's discernment.

4. I have let myself be inspired by the wealth of reflections and conversations that emerged from last year's Synod. I cannot include all those contributions here, but you can read them in the Final Document. In writing this letter, though, I have attempted to summarize those proposals I considered most significant. In this way, my words will echo the myriad voices of believers the world over who made their opinions known to the Synod. Those young people who are not believers, yet wished to share their thoughts, also raised issues that led me to ask new questions.

# CHAPTER ONE

# What Does the Word of God Have to Say About Young People?

5. Let us draw upon some of the richness of the sacred Scriptures, since they often speak of young people and of how the Lord draws near to encounter them.

## IN THE OLD TESTAMENT

6. In an age when young people were not highly regarded, some texts show that God sees them differently. Joseph, for example, was one of the youngest of his family (cf. Gen 37:2-3), yet God showed him great things in dreams and when about twenty years old he outshone all his brothers in important affairs (cf. Gen 37-47).

7. In Gideon, we see the frankness of young people, who are not used to sugar-coating reality. When told that the Lord was with him, he responded: "But if the Lord is with us, why then have all these things happened to us?" (Jg 6:13). God was not offended by that reproach, but went on to order him: "Go in this might of yours and deliver Israel!" (Jg 6:14).

8. Samuel was still a young boy, yet the Lord spoke to him. Thanks to the advice of an adult, he opened his heart to hear God's call: "Speak, Lord, for your servant is listening" (1 Sam 3:9-10). As a result, he became a great prophet who intervened at critical moments in the history of his country. King Saul was also young when the Lord called him to undertake his mission (cf. 1 Sam 9:2).

9. King David was chosen while still a boy. When the prophet Samuel was seeking the future king of Israel, a man offered as candidates his sons who were older and more experienced. Yet the prophet said that the chosen one was the young David, who was out tending the flock (cf. 1 Sam 16:6-13), for "man looks on the outward appearance, but the Lord looks on the heart" (v. 7). The glory of youth is in the heart, more than in physical strength or the impression given to others.

10. Solomon, when he had to succeed his father, felt lost and told God: "I am a mere youth, not knowing at all how to act" (1 Kg 3:7). Yet the audacity of youth moved him to ask God for wisdom and he devoted himself to his mission. Something similar happened to the prophet Jeremiah, called despite his youth to rouse his people. In his fear, he said: "Ah, Lord God! Truly I do not know how to speak, for I am only a youth" (Jer 1:6). But the Lord told him not to say that (cf. Jer 1:7), and added: "Do not be afraid of them, for I am with you to deliver you" (Jer 1:8). The devotion of the prophet Jeremiah to his mission shows what can happen when the brashness of youth is joined to the power of God.

11. A Jewish servant girl of the foreign commander Naaman intervened with faith and helped him to be cured of his illness (cf. 2 Kg 5:2-6). The young Ruth was a model of generosity in remaining beside her mother-in-law who had fallen on hard times (cf. Ru 1:1-18), yet she also showed boldness in getting ahead in life (cf. Ru 4:1-17).

## IN THE NEW TESTAMENT

12. One of Jesus' parables (cf. Lk 15:11-32) relates that a "younger" son wanted to leave his father's home for a distant land (cf. vv. 12-13). Yet his thoughts of independence turned into dissolution and excess (cf. v. 13), and he came to experience the bitterness of loneliness and poverty (cf. vv. 14-16). Nonetheless, he found the

strength to make a new start (cf. vv. 17-19) and determined to get up and return home (cf. v. 20). Young hearts are naturally ready to change, to turn back, get up and learn from life. How could anyone fail to support that son in this new resolution? Yet his older brother already had a heart grown old; he let himself be possessed by greed, selfishness and envy (Lk 15:28-30). Jesus praises the young sinner who returned to the right path over the brother who considered himself faithful, yet lacked the spirit of love and mercy.

13. Jesus, himself eternally young, wants to give us hearts that are ever young. God's word asks us to "cast out the old leaven that you may be fresh dough" (1 Cor 5:7). St. Paul invites us to strip ourselves of the "old self" and to put on a "young" self (Col 3:9-10).[1] In explaining what it means to put on that youthfulness "which is being renewed" (v. 10), he mentions "compassion, kindness, humility, meekness and patience, bearing with one another and forgiving each other if anyone has a complaint against another" (Col 3:12-13). In a word, true youth means having a heart capable of loving, whereas everything that separates us from others makes the soul grow old. And so he concludes: "above all, clothe yourselves with love, which binds everything together in perfect harmony" (Col 3:14).

14. Let us also keep in mind that Jesus had no use for adults who looked down on the young or lorded it over them. On the contrary, he insisted that "the greatest among you must become like the youngest" (Lk 22:26). For him age did not establish privileges, and being young did not imply lesser worth or dignity.

15. The word of God says that young people should be treated "as brothers" (1 Tim 5:1), and warns parents not to "provoke your children, lest they become discouraged" (Col 3:21). Young people are not meant to become discouraged; they are meant to dream great things, to seek vast horizons, to aim higher, to take on the world, to

---

1    The Greek word usually translated "new" can also mean "young."

accept challenges and to offer the best of themselves to the building of something better. That is why I constantly urge young people not to let themselves be robbed of hope; to each of them I repeat: "Let no one despise your youth" (1 Tim 4:12).

16. Nonetheless, young people are also urged "to accept the authority of those who are older" (1 Pet 5:5). The Bible never ceases to insist that profound respect be shown to the elderly, since they have a wealth of experience; they have known success and failure, life's joys and afflictions, its dreams and disappointments. In the silence of their heart, they have a store of experiences that can teach us not to make mistakes or be taken in by false promises. An ancient sage asks us to respect certain limits and to master our impulses: "Urge the younger men to be self-controlled" (Tit 2:6). It is unhelpful to buy into the cult of youth or foolishly to dismiss others simply because they are older or from another generation. Jesus tells us that the wise are able to bring forth from their store things both new and old (cf. Mt 13:52). A wise young person is open to the future, yet still capable of learning something from the experience of others.

17. In the Gospel of Mark, we find a man who, listening to Jesus speak of the commandments, says, "All these I have observed from my youth" (10:20). The Psalmist had already said the same thing: "You, O Lord, are my hope; my trust, O Lord, from my youth . . . from my youth you have taught me, and I still proclaim your wondrous deeds" (Ps 71:5, 17). We should never repent of spending our youth being good, opening our heart to the Lord, and living differently. None of this takes away from our youth but instead strengthens and renews it: "Your youth is renewed like the eagle's" (Ps 103:5). For this reason, St. Augustine could lament: "Late have I loved you, beauty ever ancient, ever new! Late have I loved you!"[2] Yet that rich man, who had been faithful to God in his youth,

---

2    *Confessions*, X, 27: PL 32, 795.

allowed the passing years to rob his dreams; he preferred to remain attached to his riches (cf. Mk 10:22).

18. On the other hand, in the Gospel of Matthew we find a young man (cf. 19:20-22) who approaches Jesus and asks if there is more that he can do (v. 20); in this, he demonstrates that youthful open-ness of spirit which seeks new horizons and great challenges. Yet his spirit was not really that young, for he had already become attached to riches and comforts. He said he wanted something more, but when Jesus asked him to be generous and distribute his goods, he realized that he could not let go of everything he had. In the end, "hearing these words, the young man went away sad" (v. 22). He had given up his youth.

19. The Gospel also speaks about a group of wise young women, who were ready and waiting, while others were distracted and slum-bering (cf. Mt 25:1-13). We can, in fact, spend our youth being distracted, skimming the surface of life, half-asleep, incapable of cultivating meaningful relationships or experiencing the deeper things in life. In this way, we can store up a paltry and unsubstantial future. Or we can spend our youth aspiring to beautiful and great things, and thus store up a future full of life and interior richness.

20. If you have lost your inner vitality, your dreams, your enthusi-asm, your optimism and your generosity, Jesus stands before you as once he stood before the dead son of the widow, and with all the power of his resurrection he urges you: "Young man, I say to you, arise!" (Lk 7:14).

21. To be sure, many other passages of the word of God can shed light on this stage of your life. We will take up some of them in the following chapters.

# CHAPTER TWO

# Jesus, Ever Young

22. Jesus is "young among the young in order to be an example for the young and to consecrate them to the Lord."[3] For this reason the Synod said that "youth is an original and stimulating stage of life, which Jesus himself experienced, thereby sanctifying it."[4]

## JESUS' YOUTH

23. The Lord "gave up his spirit" (cf. Mt 27:50) on a cross when he was little more than thirty years of age (cf. Lk 3:23). It is important to realize that Jesus was a young person. He gave his life when he was, in today's terms, a young adult. He began his public mission in the prime of life, and thus "a light dawned" (Mt 4:16) that would shine most brightly when he gave his life to the very end. That ending was not something that simply happened; rather, his entire youth, at every moment, was a precious preparation for it. "Everything in Jesus's life was a sign of his mystery";[5] indeed, "Christ's whole life is a mystery of redemption."[6]

24. The Gospel tells us nothing of Jesus' childhood, but it does recount several events of his adolescence and youth. Matthew situates the time of the Lord's youth between two events: his family's return to Nazareth after their exile, and Jesus' baptism in the Jordan, the beginning of his public ministry. The last images we have of Jesus as a child are those of a tiny refugee in Egypt (cf. Mt 2:14-15)

3  St. Irenaeus, *Adversus Hæreses*, II, 22, 4: PG 7, 784.

4  *Final Document of the Fifteenth Ordinary General Assembly of the Synod of Bishops,* no. 60. Hereafter cited as FD. The document can be found at: *http://www.vatican.va/roman_curia/synod/documents/rc_synod_doc_20181027_doc-final-instrumentum-xvassemblea-giovani_en.html.*

5  *Catechism of the Catholic Church,* no. 515.

6  Ibid., no. 517.

and repatriated in Nazareth (cf. Mt 2:19-23). Our first image of Jesus as a young adult shows him standing among the crowds on the banks of the Jordan river to be baptized by his kinsman John the Baptist, just like any other member of his people (cf. Mt 3:13-17).

25. Jesus' baptism was not like our own, which introduces us to the life of grace, but a consecration prior to his embarking on the great mission of his life. The Gospel says that at his baptism the Father rejoiced and was well pleased: "You are my beloved Son" (Lk 3:22). Jesus immediately appeared filled with the Holy Spirit, and was led by the Spirit into the desert. There he prepared to go forth to preach and to work miracles, to bring freedom and healing (cf. Lk 4:1-14). Every young person who feels called to a mission in this world is invited to hear the Father speaking those same words within his or her heart: "You are my beloved child."

26. Between these two accounts, we find another, which shows Jesus as an adolescent, when he had returned with his parents to Nazareth, after being lost and found in the Temple (cf. Lk 2:41-51). There we read that "he was obedient to them" (cf. Lk 2:51); he did not disown his family. Luke then adds that Jesus "grew in wisdom, age and grace before God and men" (cf. Lk 2:52). In a word, this was a time of preparation, when Jesus grew in his relationship with the Father and with others. St. John Paul II explained that he did not only grow physically, but that "there was also a spiritual growth in Jesus," because "the fullness of grace in Jesus was in proportion to his age: there was always a fullness, but a fullness which increased as he grew in age."[7]

27. From what the Gospel tells us, we can say that Jesus, in the years of his youth, was "training," being prepared to carry out the Father's plan. His adolescence and his youth set him on the path to that sublime mission.

---

7    Catechesis (June 27, 1990), 2-3: *Insegnamenti* 13, 1 (1990), 1680-1681.

28. In his adolescence and youth, Jesus' relationship with the Father was that of the beloved Son. Drawn to the Father, he grew up concerned for his affairs: "Did you not know that I must be about my Father's business?" (Lk 2:49). Still, it must not be thought that Jesus was a withdrawn adolescent or a self-absorbed youth. His relationships were those of a young person who shared fully in the life of his family and his people. He learned his father's trade and then replaced him as a carpenter. At one point in the Gospel he is called "the carpenter's son" (Mt 13:55) and another time simply "the carpenter" (Mk 6:3). This detail shows that he was just another young person of his town, who related normally to others. No one regarded him as unusual or set apart from others. For this very reason, once Jesus began to preach, people could not imagine where he got this wisdom: "Is this not Joseph's son?" (Lk 4:22).

29. In fact, "Jesus did not grow up in a narrow and stifling relationship with Mary and Joseph, but readily interacted with the wider family, the relatives of his parents and their friends."[8] Hence we can understand why, when he returned from his pilgrimage to Jerusalem, his parents readily thought that, as a twelve-year-old boy (cf. Lk 2:42), he was wandering freely among the crowd, even though they did not see him for an entire day: "supposing him to be in the group of travellers, they went a day's journey" (Lk 2:44). Surely, they assumed, Jesus was there, mingling with the others, joking with other young people, listening to the adults tell stories and sharing the joys and sorrows of the group. Indeed, the Greek word that Luke uses to describe the group—*synodía*—clearly evokes a larger "community on a journey" of which the Holy Family is a part. Thanks to the trust of his parents, Jesus can move freely and learn to journey with others.

---

8    Post-Synodal Apostolic Exhortation *Amoris Laetitia* (March 19, 2016), no. 182: AAS 108 (2016), 384.

# HIS YOUTH TEACHES US

30. These aspects of Jesus' life can prove inspiring for all those young people who are developing and preparing to take up their mission in life. This involves growing in a relationship with the Father, in awareness of being part of a family and a people, and in openness to being filled with the Holy Spirit and led to carry out the mission God gives them, their personal vocation. None of this should be overlooked in pastoral work with young people, lest we create projects that isolate young people from their family and the larger community, or turn them into a select few, protected from all contamination. Rather, we need projects that can strengthen them, accompany them and impel them to encounter others, to engage in generous service, in mission.

31. Jesus does not teach you, young people, from afar or from without, but from within your very youth, a youth he shares with you. It is very important for you to contemplate the young Jesus as presented in the Gospels, for he was truly one of you, and shares many of the features of your young hearts. We see this for example in the following: "Jesus had unconditional trust in the Father; he maintained friendship with his disciples, and even in moments of crisis he remained faithful to them. He showed profound compassion for the weakest, especially the poor, the sick, sinners and the excluded. He had the courage to confront the religious and political authorities of his time; he knew what it was to feel misunderstood and rejected; he experienced the fear of suffering and he knew the frailty of the Passion. He turned his gaze to the future, entrusting himself into the Father's safe hands in the strength of the Spirit. In Jesus, all the young can see themselves."[9]

32. On the other hand, Jesus is risen, and he wants to make us sharers in the new life of the resurrection. He is the true youthfulness of a world grown old, the youthfulness of a universe waiting "in

---

9    FD, no. 63.

travail" (Rom 8:22) to be clothed with his light and to live his life. With him at our side, we can drink from the true wellspring that keeps alive all our dreams, our projects, our great ideals, while impelling us to proclaim what makes life truly worthwhile. Two curious details in the Gospel of Mark show how those risen with Christ are called to authentic youth. In the Lord's passion we see a young man who wanted to follow Jesus, but in fear ran away naked (cf. 14:51-52); he lacked the strength to stake everything on following the Lord. Yet at the empty tomb, we see another young person, "dressed in a white tunic" (16:5), who tells the women not to be afraid and proclaims the joy of the resurrection (cf. 16:6-7).

33. The Lord is calling us to enkindle stars in the night of other young people. He asks you to look to the true stars, all those varied signs he gives us to guide our way, and to imitate the farmer who watches the stars before going out to plow his field. God lights up stars to help us keep walking: "The stars shine in their watches, and are glad; he calls them, and they say, 'Here we are!'" (Bar 3:34-35). Christ himself is our great light of hope and our guide in the night, for he is the "bright morning star" (Rev 22:16).

# THE YOUTH OF THE CHURCH

34. Youth is more than simply a period of time; it is a state of mind. That is why an institution as ancient as the Church can experience renewal and a return to youth at different points in her age-old history. Indeed, at the most dramatic moments of her history, she feels called to return with all her heart to her first love. Recalling this truth, the Second Vatican Council noted that, "enriched by a long and living history, and advancing toward human perfection in time and the ultimate destinies of history and of life, the Church is the real youth of the world." In her, it is always possible to encounter Christ "the companion and friend of youth."[10]

---

10   Second Vatican Ecumenical Council, *Message to Young Men and Women* (December 8, 1965): AAS 58 (1966), 18.

35. Let us ask the Lord to free the Church from those who would make her grow old, encase her in the past, hold her back or keep her at a standstill. But let us also ask him to free her from another temptation: that of thinking she is young because she accepts everything the world offers her, thinking that she is renewed because she sets her message aside and acts like everybody else. No! The Church is young when she is herself, when she receives ever anew the strength born of God's word, the Eucharist, and the daily presence of Christ and the power of his Spirit in our lives. The Church is young when she shows herself capable of constantly returning to her source.

36. Certainly, as members of the Church, we should not stand apart from others. All should regard us as friends and neighbors, like the apostles, who "enjoyed the good will of all the people" (Acts 2:47; cf. 4:21, 33; 5:13). Yet at the same time we must dare to be different, to point to ideals other than those of this world, testifying to the beauty of generosity, service, purity, perseverance, forgiveness, fidelity to our personal vocation, prayer, the pursuit of justice and the common good, love for the poor, and social friendship.

37. Christ's Church can always yield to the temptation to lose enthusiasm because she no longer hears the Lord calling her to take the risk of faith, to give her all without counting the dangers; she can be tempted to revert to seeking a false, worldly form of security. Young people can help keep her young. They can stop her from becoming corrupt; they can keep her moving forward, prevent her from being proud and sectarian, help her to be poorer and to bear better witness, to take the side of the poor and the outcast, to fight for justice and humbly to let herself be challenged. Young people can offer the Church the beauty of youth by renewing her ability to

"rejoice with new beginnings, to give unreservedly of herself, to be renewed and to set out for ever greater accomplishments."[11]

38. Those of us who are no longer young need to find ways of keeping close to the voices and concerns of young people. "Drawing together creates the conditions for the Church to become a place of dialogue and a witness to life-giving fraternity."[12] We need to make more room for the voices of young people to be heard: "listening makes possible an exchange of gifts in a context of empathy . . . At the same time, it sets the conditions for a preaching of the Gospel that can touch the heart truly, decisively and fruitfully."[13]

## A CHURCH ATTENTIVE TO THE SIGNS OF THE TIMES

39. "Even though to many young people, God, religion and the Church seem empty words, they are sensitive to the figure of Jesus when he is presented in an attractive and effective way."[14] Consequently, the Church should not be excessively caught up in herself but instead, and above all, reflect Jesus Christ. This means humbly acknowledging that some things concretely need to change, and if that is to happen, she needs to appreciate the vision but also the criticisms of young people.

40. The Synod recognized that "a substantial number of young people, for all sorts of reasons, do not ask the Church for anything because they do not see her as significant for their lives. Some even ask expressly to be left alone, as they find the presence of the Church a nuisance, even an irritant. This request does not always stem from uncritical or impulsive contempt. It can also have serious and understandable reasons: sexual and financial scandals; a clergy ill-prepared to engage effectively with the sensitivities of the young;

---

11   Ibid.

12   FD, no. 1.

13   Ibid., no. 8.

14   Ibid., no. 50.

lack of care in homily preparation and the presentation of the word of God; the passive role assigned to the young within the Christian community; the Church's difficulty in explaining her doctrine and ethical positions to contemporary society."[15]

41. Although many young people are happy to see a Church that is humble yet confident in her gifts and capable of offering fair and fraternal criticism, others want a Church that listens more, that does more than simply condemn the world. They do not want to see a Church that is silent and afraid to speak, but neither one that is always battling obsessively over two or three issues. To be credible to young people, there are times when she needs to regain her humility and simply listen, recognizing that what others have to say can provide some light to help her better understand the Gospel. A Church always on the defensive, which loses her humility and stops listening to others, which leaves no room for questions, loses her youth and turns into a museum. How, then, will she be able to respond to the dreams of young people? Even if she possesses the truth of the Gospel, this does not mean that she has completely understood it; rather, she is called to keep growing in her grasp of that inexhaustible treasure.[16]

42. For example, a Church that is overly fearful and tied to its structures can be invariably critical of efforts to defend the rights of women, and constantly point out the risks and the potential errors of those demands. Instead, a living Church can react by being attentive to the legitimate claims of those women who seek greater justice and equality. A living Church can look back on history and acknowledge a fair share of male authoritarianism, domination, various forms of enslavement, abuse and sexist violence. With this outlook, she can support the call to respect women's rights, and offer convinced support for greater reciprocity between males

---

15   Ibid., no. 53.

16   Cf. Second Vatican Ecumenical Council, Dogmatic Constitution on Divine Revelation *Dei Verbum*, no. 8.

and females, while not agreeing with everything some feminist groups propose. Along these lines, the Synod sought to renew the Church's commitment "against all discrimination and violence on sexual grounds."[17] That is the response of a Church that stays young and lets herself be challenged and spurred on by the sensitivities of young people.

## MARY, THE YOUNG WOMAN OF NAZARETH

43. In the heart of the Church, Mary shines forth. She is the supreme model for a youthful Church that seeks to follow Christ with enthusiasm and docility. While still very young, she accepted the message of the angel, yet she was not afraid to ask questions (cf. Lk 1:34). With open heart and soul, she replied, "Behold, I am the handmaid of the Lord" (Lk 1:38).

44. "We are always struck by the strength of the young Mary's 'yes,' the strength in those words, 'be it done,' that she spoke to the angel. This was no merely passive or resigned acceptance, or a faint 'yes,' as if to say, 'Well, let's give it a try and see what happens.' Mary did not know the words, 'Let's see what happens.' She was determined; she knew what was at stake and she said 'yes' without thinking twice. Hers was the 'yes' of someone prepared to be committed, someone willing to take a risk, ready to stake everything she had, with no more security than the certainty of knowing that she was the bearer of a promise. So I ask each one of you: do you see yourselves as the bearers of a promise? What promise is present in my heart that I can take up? Mary's mission would undoubtedly be difficult, but the challenges that lay ahead were no reason to say 'no.' Things would get complicated, of course, but not in the same way as happens when cowardice paralyzes us because things are not clear or sure in advance. Mary did not take out an insurance policy! She took the risk, and for this reason she is strong, she is an

---

17    FD, no. 150.

15

'influencer,' the 'influencer' of God. Her 'yes and her desire to serve were stronger than any doubts or difficulties.'"[18]

45. Without yielding to evasions or illusions, "she accompanied the suffering of her Son; she supported him by her gaze and protected him with her heart. She shared his suffering, yet was not overwhelmed by it. She was the woman of strength who uttered her 'yes,' who supports and accompanies, protects and embraces. She is the great guardian of hope . . . From her, we learn how to say 'yes' to the stubborn endurance and creativity of those who, undaunted, are ever ready to start over again."[19]

46. Mary was a young woman whose heart overflowed with joy (cf. Lk 1:47), whose eyes, reflecting the light of the Holy Spirit, looked at life with faith and treasured all things in her youthful heart (cf. Lk 2:19, 51). She was energetic, ready to set out immediately once she knew that her cousin needed her. She did not think about her own plans, but went "with haste" to the hill country (Lk 1:39).

47. When her young son needed protection, Mary set out with Joseph to a distant land (cf. Mt 2:13-14). She also joined the disciples in awaiting the outpouring of the Holy Spirit (cf. Acts 1:14). In her presence, a young Church was born, as the apostles went forth to give birth to a new world (cf. Acts 2:4-11).

48. Today, Mary is the Mother who watches over us, her children, on our journey through life, often weary and in need, anxious that the light of hope not fail. For that is our desire: that the light of hope never fail. Mary our Mother looks to this pilgrim people: a youthful people whom she loves, and who seek her in the silence of their hearts amid all the noise, the chatter and the distractions of

---

18 *Address at the Vigil, XXXIV World Youth Day in Panama* (January 26, 2019): *L'Osservatore Romano*, January 28-29, 2019, 6.

19 *Prayer at the Conclusion of the Way of the Cross, XXXIV World Youth Day in Panama* (January 26, 2019): *L'Osservatore Romano*, January 27, 2019, 12.

the journey. Under the gaze of our Mother, there is room only for the silence of hope. Thus Mary illumines anew our youth.

## YOUNG SAINTS

49. The heart of the Church is also full of young saints who devoted their lives to Christ, many of them even to dying a martyr's death. They were precious reflections of the young Christ; their radiant witness encourages us and awakens us from our lethargy. The Synod pointed out that "many young saints have allowed the features of youth to shine forth in all their beauty, and in their day they have been real prophets of change. Their example shows what the young are capable of, when they open themselves up to encounter Christ."[20]

50. "Through the holiness of the young, the Church can renew her spiritual ardor and her apostolic vigor. The balm of holiness generated by the good lives of so many young people can heal the wounds of the Church and of the world, bringing us back to that fullness of love to which we have always been called: young saints inspire us to return to our first love (cf. Rev 2:4)."[21] Some saints never reached adulthood, yet they showed us that there is another way to spend our youth. Let us recall at least some of them who, each in his or her own way, and at different periods of history, lived lives of holiness.

51. In the third century, St. Sebastian was a young captain of the Praetorian Guard. It is said that he spoke constantly of Christ and tried to convert his companions, to the point that he was ordered to renounce his faith. Since he refused, he was shot with arrows, yet he survived and continued to proclaim Christ fearlessly. In the end, Sebastian was flogged to death.

---

20  FD, no. 65.

21  Ibid., no. 167.

52. St. Francis of Assisi, while very young and full of great dreams, heard Jesus' call to become poor like him and to rebuild the Church by his witness. He joyfully renounced everything he had and is now the saint of universal fraternity, the brother of all. He praised the Lord for his creatures. Francis died in 1226.

53. St. Joan of Arc was born in 1412. She was a young peasant girl who, despite her tender years, fought to defend France from invaders. Misunderstood for her demeanor, her actions and her way of living the faith, Joan was burned at the stake.

54. Bl. Andrew Phû Yên was a young Vietnamese man of the seventeenth century. He was a catechist and assisted the missionaries. He was imprisoned for his faith, and since he refused to renounce it, he was killed. Andrew died uttering the name of Jesus.

55. In that same century, St. Kateri Tekakwitha, a young native of North America, was persecuted for her faith and, to escape, walked over three hundred kilometres in the wilderness. Kateri consecrated herself to God and died saying: "Jesus, I love you!"

56. St. Dominic Savio offered all his sufferings to Mary. When St. John Bosco taught him that holiness involves being constantly joyful, he opened his heart to a contagious joy. He wanted to be close to the most abandoned and infirm of his fellow young people. Dominic died in 1857 at fourteen years of age, saying: "What a wondrous thing I am experiencing!"

57. St. Thérèse of the Child Jesus was born in 1873. At fifteen years of age, having overcome many difficulties, she succeeded in entering the Carmelite convent. Thérèse lived the little way of complete trust in the Lord's love and determined to fan with her prayers the fire of love burning in the heart of the Church.

58. Bl. Ceferino Namuncurá was a young Argentinian, the son of the chief of a remote tribe of indigenous peoples. He became

a Salesian seminarian, filled with the desire to return to his tribe, bringing Jesus Christ to them. Ceferino died in 1905.

59. Bl. Isidore Bakanja was a layman from the Congo who bore witness to his faith. He was tortured at length for having proposed Christianity to other young people. Forgiving his executioner, Isidore died in 1909.

60. Bl. Pier Giorgio Frassati, who died in 1925, "was a young man filled with a joy that swept everything along with it, a joy that also overcame many difficulties in his life."[22] Pier Giorgio said that he wanted to return the love of Jesus that he received in Holy Communion by visiting and helping the poor.

61. Bl. Marcel Callo was a young French man who died in 1945. Marcel was imprisoned in a concentration camp in Austria, where he strengthened his fellow prisoners in faith amid harsh labors.

62. The young Bl. Chiara Badano, who died in 1990, "experienced how pain could be transfigured by love . . . The key to her peace and joy was her complete trust in the Lord and the acceptance of her illness as a mysterious expression of his will for her sake and that of others."[23]

63. May these and so many other young people who perhaps in silence and hiddenness lived the Gospel to the full, intercede for the Church, so that she may be full of joyous, courageous and committed young people who can offer the world new testimonies of holiness.

---

22   St. John Paul II, *Address to Young People in Turin* (April 13, 1980), no. 4: *Insegnamenti* 3, 1 (1980), 905.

23   Benedict XVI, *Message for the XXVII World Youth Day* (March 15, 2012): AAS 194 (2012), 359.

## CHAPTER THREE

# You Are the "Now" of God

64. After this brief look at the word of God, we cannot just say that young people are the future of our world. They are its present; even now, they are helping to enrich it. Young people are no longer children. They are at a time of life when they begin to assume a number of responsibilities, sharing alongside adults in the growth of the family, society and the Church. Yet the times are changing, leading us to ask: What are today's young people really like? What is going on in their lives?

## IN POSITIVE TERMS

65. The Synod recognized that the members of the Church do not always take the approach of Jesus. Rather than listening to young people attentively, "all too often, there is a tendency to provide pre-packaged answers and ready-made solutions, without allowing their real questions to emerge and facing the challenges they pose."[24] Yet once the Church sets aside narrow preconceptions and listens carefully to the young, this empathy enriches her, for "it allows young people to make their own contribution to the community, helping it to appreciate new sensitivities and to consider new questions."[25]

66. We adults can often be tempted to list all the problems and failings of today's young people. Perhaps some will find it praiseworthy that we seem so expert in discerning difficulties and dangers. But what would be the result of such an attitude? Greater distance, less closeness, less mutual assistance.

---

24  FD, no. 8.

25  Ibid.

67. Anyone called to be a parent, pastor or guide to young people must have the farsightedness to appreciate the little flame that continues to burn, the fragile reed that is shaken but not broken (cf. Is 42:3). The ability to discern pathways where others only see walls, to recognize potential where others see only peril. That is how God the Father see things; he knows how to cherish and nurture the seeds of goodness sown in the hearts of the young. Each young person's heart should thus be considered "holy ground," a bearer of seeds of divine life, before which we must "take off our shoes" in order to draw near and enter more deeply into the Mystery.

## MANY WAYS OF BEING YOUNG

68. We might attempt to draw a picture of young people today, but first I would echo the Synod Fathers, who noted that "the makeup of the Synod brought out the presence and contribution of many different regions of the world, and highlighted the beauty of our being a universal Church. In a context of growing globalization, the Synod Fathers wanted the many differences of contexts and cultures, even within individual countries, to be duly emphasized. The worlds of today's 'youth' are so many that in some countries one tends to speak of 'young people' in the plural. The age group considered by the Synod (16-29 years) does not represent a homogeneous category, but is composed of distinct groups, each with its own life experience."[26]

69. From a demographic standpoint too, some countries have many young people, whereas others have a very low birth rate. "A further differentiating factor is historical: there are countries and continents of ancient Christian tradition, whose culture is indelibly marked by a memory that cannot be lightly dismissed, while other countries and continents are characterized by other religious traditions, where Christianity is a minority presence—and at times a

---

26   Ibid., no. 10.

recent one. In other places still, Christian communities, and young people who belong to them, experience persecution."[27] There is also a need to distinguish young people "with access to the growing opportunities offered by globalization from those who live on the fringes of society or in rural areas, and find themselves excluded or discarded."[28]

70. There are many more differences, which it would be difficult to examine here. In any event, I see no need for a detailed analysis of today's young people, their lives and their experiences. At the same time, since I do not want to neglect that reality, I will briefly summarize some contributions received before the Synod and others that I heard in the course of our meetings.

# SOME EXPERIENCES OF YOUNG PEOPLE

71. Youth is not something to be analyzed in the abstract. Indeed, "youth" does not exist: there exist only young people, each with the reality of his or her own life. In today's rapidly changing world, many of those lives are exposed to suffering and manipulation.

## *LIVING IN A WORLD IN CRISIS*

72. The Synod Fathers acknowledged with sorrow that "many young people today live in war zones and experience violence in countless different forms: kidnapping, extortion, organized crime, human trafficking, slavery and sexual exploitation, wartime rape, and so forth. Other young people, because of their faith, struggle to find their place in society and endure various kinds of persecution, even murder. Many young people, whether by force or lack of alternatives, live by committing crimes and acts of violence: child soldiers, armed criminal gangs, drug trafficking, terrorism, and so on. This violence destroys many young lives. Abuse and addiction,

---

27  Ibid., no. 11.

28  Ibid., no. 12.

together with violence and wrongdoing, are some of the reasons that send young people to prison, with a higher incidence in certain ethnic and social groups."[29]

73. Many young people are taken in by ideologies, used and exploited as cannon fodder or a strike force to destroy, terrify or ridicule others. Worse yet, many of them end up as individualists, hostile and distrustful of others; in this way, they become an easy target for the brutal and destructive strategies of political groups or economic powers.

74. "Even more numerous in the world are young people who suffer forms of marginalization and social exclusion for religious, ethnic or economic reasons. Let us not forget the difficult situation of adolescents and young people who become pregnant, the scourge of abortion, the spread of HIV, various forms of addiction (drugs, gambling, pornography and so forth), and the plight of street children without homes, families or economic resources."[30] In the case of women, these situations are doubly painful and difficult.

75. As a Church, may we never fail to weep before these tragedies of our young. May we never become inured to them, for anyone incapable of tears cannot be a mother. We want to weep so that society itself can be more of a mother, so that in place of killing it can learn to give birth, to become a promise of life. We weep when we think of all those young people who have already lost their lives due to poverty and violence, and we ask society to learn to be a caring mother. None of this pain goes away; it stays with us, because the harsh reality can no longer be concealed. The worst thing we can do is adopt that worldly spirit whose solution is simply to anaesthetize young people with other messages, with other distractions, with trivial pursuits.

---

29   Ibid., no. 41.

30   Ibid., no. 42.

76. Perhaps "those of us who have a reasonably comfortable life don't know how to weep. Some realities in life are only seen with eyes cleansed by tears. I would like each of you to ask yourself this question: Can I weep? Can I weep when I see a child who is starving, on drugs or on the street, homeless, abandoned, mistreated or exploited as a slave by society? Or is my weeping only the self-centered whining of those who cry because they want something else?"[31] Try to learn to weep for all those young people less fortunate than yourselves. Weeping is also an expression of mercy and compassion. If tears do not come, ask the Lord to give you the grace to weep for the sufferings of others. Once you can weep, then you will be able to help others from the heart.

77. At times, the hurt felt by some young people is heart-rending, a pain too deep for words. They can only tell God how much they are suffering, and how hard it is for them to keep going, since they no longer believe in anyone. Yet in that sorrowful plea, the words of Jesus make themselves heard: "Blessed are those who mourn, for they shall be comforted" (Mt 5:4). Some young men and women were able to move forward because they heard that divine promise. May all young people who are suffering feel the closeness of a Christian community that can reflect those words by its actions, its embrace and its concrete help.

78. It is true that people in power offer some assistance, but often it comes at a high price. In many poor countries, economic aid provided by some richer countries or international agencies is usually tied to the acceptance of Western views of sexuality, marriage, life or social justice. This ideological colonization is especially harmful to the young. We also see how a certain kind of advertising teaches young people to be perpetually dissatisfied and contributes to the throwaway culture, in which young people themselves end up being discarded.

---

31  *Address to Young People in Manila* (January 18, 2015): *L'Osservatore Romano*, January 19-20, 2015, 7.

79. Our present-day culture exploits the image of the young. Beauty is associated with a youthful appearance, cosmetic treatments that hide the traces of time. Young bodies are constantly advertised as a means of selling products. The ideal of beauty is youth, but we need to realize that this has very little to do with young people. It only means that adults want to snatch youth for themselves, not that they respect, love and care for young people.

80. Some young people "find family traditions oppressive and they flee from them under the impulse of a globalized culture that at times leaves them without points of reference. In other parts of the world, even more than generational conflict between young people and adults, there is mutual estrangement. Sometimes adults fail, or do not even try, to hand on the basic values of life, or they try to imitate young people, thus inverting the relationship between generations. The relationship between young people and adults thus risks remaining on the affective level, leaving its educational and cultural aspects untouched."[32] What harm this does to young people, even though some do not notice it! Young people themselves have remarked how enormously difficult this makes the transmission of the faith "in some countries without freedom of speech, where young people are prevented from attending Church."[33]

## Desires, Hurts and Longings

81. Young people are aware that the body and sexuality have an essential importance for their lives and for their process of growth in identity. Yet in a world that constantly exalts sexuality, maintaining a healthy relationship with one's body and a serene affective life is not easy. For this and other reasons, sexual morality often tends to be a source of "incomprehension and alienation from the Church, inasmuch as she is viewed as a place of judgment

---

32  FD, no. 34.

33  *Document of the Pre-Synodal Meeting in Preparation for the XV Ordinary General Assembly of the Synod of Bishops*, Rome (March 24, 2018), I, 1.

and condemnation." Nonetheless, young people also express "an explicit desire to discuss questions concerning the difference between male and female identity, reciprocity between men and women, and homosexuality."[34]

82. In our times, "advances in the sciences and in biomedical technologies have powerfully influenced perceptions about the body, leading to the idea that it is open to unlimited modification. The capacity to intervene in DNA, the possibility of inserting artificial elements into organisms (cyborgs) and the development of the neurosciences represent a great resource, but at the same time they raise serious anthropological and ethical questions."[35] They can make us forget that life is a gift, and that we are creatures with innate limits, open to exploitation by those who wield technological power.[36] "Moreover, in some youth circles, there is a growing fascination with risk-taking behavior as a means of self-exploration, seeking powerful emotions and gaining attention . . . These realities, to which young generations are exposed, are an obstacle to their serene growth in maturity."[37]

83. Young people also experience setbacks, disappointments and profoundly painful memories. Often they feel "the hurt of past failures, frustrated desires, experiences of discrimination and injustice, of feeling unloved and unaccepted." Then too "there are moral wounds, the burden of past errors, a sense of guilt for having made mistakes."[38] Jesus makes his presence felt amid these crosses borne by young people; he offers them his friendship, his consolation and his healing companionship. The Church wants to be his instrument on this path to interior healing and peace of heart.

---

34  FD, no. 39.

35  Ibid., no. 37.

36  Cf. Encyclical Letter *Laudato Si'* (May 24, 2015), no. 106: AAS 107 (2015), 889-890.

37  FD, no. 37.

38  Ibid., no. 67.

84. In some young people, we can see a desire for God, albeit still vague and far from knowledge of the God of revelation. In others, we can glimpse an ideal of human fraternity, which is no small thing. Many have a genuine desire to develop their talents in order to offer something to our world. In some, we see a special artistic sensitivity, or a yearning for harmony with nature. In others, perhaps, a great need to communicate. In many of them, we encounter a deep desire to live life differently. In all of this, we can find real starting points, inner resources open to a word of incentive, wisdom and encouragement.

85. The Synod dealt in particular with three areas of utmost importance. Here I would like to quote its conclusions, while recognizing that they call for greater analysis and the development of a more adequate and effective ability to respond.

## THE DIGITAL ENVIRONMENT

86. "The digital environment is characteristic of the contemporary world. Broad swathes of humanity are immersed in it in an ordinary and continuous manner. It is no longer merely a question of 'using' instruments of communication, but of living in a highly digitalized culture that has had a profound impact on ideas of time and space, on our self-understanding, our understanding of others and the world, and our ability to communicate, learn, be informed and enter into relationship with others. An approach to reality that privileges images over listening and reading has influenced the way people learn and the development of their critical sense."[39]

87. The web and social networks have created a new way to communicate and bond. They are "a public square where the young spend much of their time and meet one another easily, even though not all have equal access to it, particularly in some regions of the world. They provide an extraordinary opportunity for dialogue, encounter

39  Ibid., no. 21.

and exchange between persons, as well as access to information and knowledge. Moreover, the digital world is one of social and political engagement and active citizenship, and it can facilitate the circulation of independent information providing effective protection for the most vulnerable and publicizing violations of their rights. In many countries, the internet and social networks already represent a firmly established forum for reaching and involving young people, not least in pastoral initiatives and activities."[40]

88. Yet to understand this phenomenon as a whole, we need to realize that, like every human reality, it has its share of limitations and deficiencies. It is not healthy to confuse communication with mere virtual contact. Indeed, "the digital environment is also one of loneliness, manipulation, exploitation and violence, even to the extreme case of the 'dark web.' Digital media can expose people to the risk of addiction, isolation and gradual loss of contact with concrete reality, blocking the development of authentic interpersonal relationships. New forms of violence are spreading through social media, for example cyberbullying. The internet is also a channel for spreading pornography and the exploitation of persons for sexual purposes or through gambling."[41]

89. It should not be forgotten that "there are huge economic interests operating in the digital world, capable of exercising forms of control as subtle as they are invasive, creating mechanisms for the manipulation of consciences and of the democratic process. The way many platforms work often ends up favoring encounter between persons who think alike, shielding them from debate. These closed circuits facilitate the spread of fake news and false information, fomenting prejudice and hate. The proliferation of fake news is the expression of a culture that has lost its sense of truth and bends the facts to suit particular interests. The reputation of individuals is put

---

40   Ibid., no. 22.
41   Ibid., no. 23.

in jeopardy through summary trials conducted online. The Church and her pastors are not exempt from this phenomenon."[42]

90. A document prepared on the eve of the Synod by three hundred young people worldwide pointed out that "online relationships can become inhuman. Digital spaces blind us to the vulnerability of another human being and prevent us from our own self-reflection. Problems like pornography distort a young person's perception of human sexuality. Technology used in this way creates a delusional parallel reality that ignores human dignity."[43] For many people, immersion in the virtual world has brought about a kind of "digital migration," involving withdrawal from their families and their cultural and religious values, and entrance into a world of loneliness and of self-invention, with the result that they feel rootless even while remaining physically in one place. The fresh and exuberant lives of young people who want to affirm their personality today confront a new challenge: that of interacting with a real and virtual world that they enter alone, as if setting foot on an undiscovered global continent. Young people today are the first to have to effect this synthesis between what is personal, what is distinctive to their respective cultures, and what is global. This means that they must find ways to pass from virtual contact to good and healthy communication.

## MIGRANTS AS AN EPITOME OF OUR TIME

91. How can we fail to think of all those young people affected by movements of migration? "Migration, considered globally, is a structural phenomenon, and not a passing emergency. It may occur within one country or between different countries. The Church's concern is focused especially on those fleeing from war, violence, political or religious persecution, from natural disasters including

---

42   Ibid., no. 24.

43   *Document of the Pre-Synodal Meeting in Preparation for the XV Ordinary General Assembly of the Synod of Bishops*, Rome (March 24, 2018), I, 4.

those caused by climate change, and from extreme poverty. Many of them are young. In general, they are seeking opportunities for themselves and their families. They dream of a better future and they want to create the conditions for achieving it."[44] Migrants "remind us of a basic aspect of our faith, that we are 'strangers and exiles on the earth' (Heb 11:13)."[45]

92. Other migrants are "attracted by Western culture, sometimes with unrealistic expectations that expose them to grave disappointments. Unscrupulous traffickers, frequently linked to drug cartels or arms cartels, exploit the weakness of migrants, who too often experience violence, trafficking, psychological and physical abuse and untold sufferings on their journey. Nor must we overlook the particular vulnerability of migrants who are unaccompanied minors, or the situation of those compelled to spend many years in refugee camps, or of those who remain trapped for a long time in transit countries, without being able to pursue a course of studies or to use their talents. In some host countries, migration causes fear and alarm, often fomented and exploited for political ends. This can lead to a xenophobic mentality, as people close in on themselves, and this needs to be addressed decisively."[46]

93. "Young migrants experience separation from their place of origin, and often a cultural and religious uprooting as well. Fragmentation is also felt by the communities they leave behind, which lose their most vigorous and enterprising elements, and by families, especially when one or both of the parents migrates, leaving the children in the country of origin. The Church has an important role as a point of reference for the young members of these divided families. However, the stories of migrants are also stories of encounter between individuals and between cultures. For the

---

44   FD, no. 25.

45   Ibid.

46   Ibid., no. 26.

communities and societies to which they come, migrants bring an opportunity for enrichment and the integral human development of all. Initiatives of welcome involving the Church have an important role from this perspective; they can bring new life to the communities capable of undertaking them."[47]

94. "Given the varied backgrounds of the Synod Fathers, the discussion of migrants benefited from a great variety of approaches, particularly from countries of departure and countries of arrival. Grave concern was also expressed by Churches whose members feel forced to escape war and persecution and by others who see in these forced migrations a threat to their survival. The very fact that the Church can embrace all these varied perspectives allows her to play a prophetic role in society with regard to the issue of migration."[48] In a special way, I urge young people not to play into the hands of those who would set them against other young people, newly arrived in their countries, and who would encourage them to view the latter as a threat, and not possessed of the same inalienable dignity as every other human being.

# ENDING EVERY FORM OF ABUSE

95. Recently, urgent appeals have been made for us to hear the cry of the victims of different kinds of abuse perpetrated by some bishops, priests, religious and laypersons. These sins cause their victims "sufferings that can last a lifetime and that no repentance can remedy. This phenomenon is widespread in society and it also affects the Church and represents a serious obstacle to her mission."[49]

96. It is true that "the scourge of the sexual abuse of minors is, and historically has been, a widespread phenomenon in all cultures and societies," especially within families and in various institutions; its

---

47    Ibid., no. 27.

48    Ibid., no. 28.

49    Ibid., no. 29.

extent has become known primarily "thanks to changes in public opinion." Even so, this problem, while it is universal and "gravely affects our societies as a whole . . . is in no way less monstrous when it takes place within the Church." Indeed, "in people's justified anger, the Church sees the reflection of the wrath of God, betrayed and insulted."[50]

97. "The Synod reaffirms the firm commitment made to adopting rigorous preventative measures intended to avoid the recurrence [of these crimes], starting with the selection and formation of those to whom tasks of responsibility and education will be entrusted."[51] At the same time, the determination to apply the "actions and sanctions that are so necessary" must be reiterated.[52] And all this with the grace of Christ. There can be no turning back.

98. "Abuse exists in various forms: the abuse of power, the abuse of conscience, sexual and financial abuse. Clearly, the ways of exercising authority that make all this possible have to be eradicated, and the irresponsibility and lack of transparency with which so many cases have been handled have to be challenged. The desire to dominate, lack of dialogue and transparency, forms of double life, spiritual emptiness, as well as psychological weaknesses, are the terrain on which corruption thrives."[53] Clericalism is a constant temptation on the part of priests who see "the ministry they have received as a power to be exercised, rather than a free and generous service to be offered. It makes us think that we belong to a group that has all the answers and no longer needs to listen or has anything to

---

50   *Address at the Conclusion of the Meeting on the Protection of Minors in the Church* (February 24, 2019): *L'Osservatore Romano*, February 25-26, 2019, 10.

51   FD, no. 29.

52   *Letter to the People of God* (August 20, 2018), 2: *L'Osservatore Romano*, August 21-21, 2018, 7.

53   FD, no. 30.

learn."[54] Doubtless, such clericalism can make consecrated persons lose respect for the sacred and inalienable worth of each person and of his or her freedom.

99. Together with the Synod Fathers, I wish to thank, with gratitude and affection, "those who had the courage to report the evil they experienced: they help the Church to acknowledge what happened and the need to respond decisively."[55] Particular gratitude is also due for "the generous commitment of countless lay persons, priests, consecrated men and women, and bishops who daily devote themselves with integrity and dedication to the service of the young. Their efforts are like a great forest that quietly grows. Many of the young people present at the Synod also expressed gratitude to those who have accompanied them and they emphasized the great need for adults who can serve as points of reference."[56]

100. Thank God, those who committed these horrible crimes are not the majority of priests, who carry out their ministry with fidelity and generosity. I ask young people to let themselves be inspired by this vast majority. And if you see a priest at risk, because he has lost the joy of his ministry, or seeks affective compensation, or is taking the wrong path, remind him of his commitment to God and his people, remind him of the Gospel and urge him to hold to his course. In this way, you will contribute greatly to something fundamental: preventing these atrocities from being repeated. This dark cloud also challenges all young people who love Jesus Christ and his Church: they can be a source of great healing if they employ their great capacity to bring about renewal, to urge and demand consistent witness, to keep dreaming and coming up with new ideas.

---

54  *Address at the Opening of the XV Ordinary General Assembly of the Synod of Bishops* (October 3, 2018): *L'Osservatore Romano,* October 5, 2018, 8.

55  FD, no. 31.

56  Ibid.

101. Nor is this the only sin of the members of the Church; her long history is not without its shadows. Our sins are before the eyes of everyone; they appear all too clearly in the lines on the age-old face of the Church, our Mother and Teacher. For two thousand years she has advanced on her pilgrim way, sharing "the joys and the hopes, the grief and anguish"[57] of all humanity. She has made this journey as she is, without cosmetic surgery of any kind. She is not afraid to reveal the sins of her members, which some try at times to hide, before the burning light of the word of the Gospel, which cleanses and purifies. Nor does she stop reciting each day, in shame: "Have mercy on me, Lord, in your kindness . . . my sin is always before me" (Ps 51:3, 5). Still, let us never forget that we must not abandon our Mother when she is wounded, but stand beside her, so that she can summon up all her strength and all her ability to begin ever anew.

102. In the midst of this tragedy, which rightly pains us, "the Lord Jesus, who never abandons his Church, offers her the strength and the means to set out on a new path."[58] This dark moment, "not without the valuable help of the young, can truly be an opportunity for a reform of epoch-making significance,"[59] opening us to a new Pentecost and inaugurating a new stage of purification and change capable of renewing the Church's youth. Young people will be all the more helpful if they feel fully a part of the "holy and patient, faithful People of God, borne up and enlivened by the Holy Spirit," for "it will be precisely this holy People of God to liberate us from the plague of clericalism, which is the fertile ground for all these disgraces."[60]

---

57    Second Vatican Ecumenical Council, Pastoral Constitution on the Church in the Modern World *Gaudium et Spes*, no. 1.

58    FD, no. 31.

59    Ibid.

60    *Address at the Conclusion of the Meeting on the Protection of Minors in the Church* (February 24, 2019): *L'Osservatore Romano*, February 25-26, 2019, 11.

# A WAY OUT

103. In this chapter, I have taken time to look at the reality of young people in today's world. Some other aspects will be dealt with in the following chapters. As I have said, I do not claim to be exhaustive in this analysis. I encourage communities to examine, respectfully and seriously, the situation of their young people, in order to find the most fitting ways of providing them with pastoral care. At the same time, I do not want to end this chapter without addressing some words to each of you.

104. I remind you of the good news we received as a gift on the morning of the resurrection: that in all the dark or painful situations that we mentioned, there is a way out. For example, it is true that the digital world can expose you to the risk of self-absorption, isolation and empty pleasure. But don't forget that there are young people even there who show creativity and even genius. That was the case with Venerable Carlo Acutis.

105. Carlo was well aware that the whole apparatus of communications, advertising and social networking can be used to lull us, to make us addicted to consumerism and buying the latest thing on the market, obsessed with our free time, caught up in negativity. Yet he knew how to use the new communications technology to transmit the Gospel, to communicate values and beauty.

106. Carlo didn't fall into the trap. He saw that many young people, wanting to be different, really end up being like everyone else, running after whatever the powerful set before them with the mechanisms of consumerism and distraction. In this way they do not bring forth the gifts the Lord has given them; they do not offer the world those unique personal talents that God has given to each of them. As a result, Carlo said, "everyone is born as an original, but many people end up dying as photocopies." Don't let that happen to you!

107. Don't let them rob you of hope and joy, or drug you into becoming a slave to their interests. Dare to be more, because who you are is more important than any possession. What good are possessions or appearances? You can become what God your Creator knows you are, if only you realize that you are called to something greater. Ask the help of the Holy Spirit and confidently aim for the great goal of holiness. In this way, you will not be a photocopy. You will be fully yourself.

108. If this is to happen, you need to realize one basic truth: being young is not only about pursuing fleeting pleasures and superficial achievements. If the years of your youth are to serve their purpose in life, they must be a time of generous commitment, whole-hearted dedication, and sacrifices that are difficult but ultimately fruitful. As a great poet put it:

> "If to regain what I regained,
> I first had to lose what I lost;
> If to achieve what I achieved,
> I had to endure what I endured;
> If to be in love now
> First I had to be hurt,
> I consider what I suffered well suffered,
> I consider what I wept for as well wept for.
> Because in the end I came to see
> That we do not really enjoy what we enjoyed
> Unless we have suffered for it.
> For in the end I realized
> That the blossoms on the tree
> Draw life from what lies buried beneath."[61]

109. If you are young in years, but feel weak, weary or disillusioned, ask Jesus to renew you. With him, hope never fails. You can do the same if you feel overwhelmed by vices, bad habits, selfishness

---

61   Francisco Luis Bernárdez, "Soneto," in *Cielo de tierra*, Buenos Aires, 1937.

or unhealthy pastimes. Jesus, brimming with life, wants to help you make your youth worthwhile. In this way, you will not deprive the world of the contribution that you alone can make, in all your uniqueness and originality.

110. Yet let me also remind you that, "when we live apart from others, it is very difficult to fight against concupiscence, the snares and temptations of the devil, and the selfishness of the world. Bombarded as we are by so many enticements, we can grow too isolated, lose our sense of reality and inner clarity, and easily succumb."[62] This is especially the case with young people, for whenever you are united, you have marvelous strength. Whenever you are enthused about life in common, you are capable of great sacrifices for others and for the community. Isolation, on the other hand, saps our strength and exposes us to the worst evils of our time.

---

62   Apostolic Exhortation *Gaudete et Exsultate* (March 19, 2018), no. 140.

## CHAPTER FOUR

# A Great Message for All Young People

111. Putting all else aside, I now wish to speak to young people about what is essential, the one thing we should never keep quiet about. It is a message containing three great truths that all of us need constantly to keep hearing.

## A GOD WHO IS LOVE

112. The very first truth I would tell each of you is this: "God loves you." It makes no difference whether you have already heard it or not. I want to remind you of it. God loves you. Never doubt this, whatever may happen to you in life. At every moment, you are infinitely loved.

113. Perhaps your experience of fatherhood has not been the best. Your earthly father may have been distant or absent, or harsh and domineering. Or maybe he was just not the father you needed. I don't know. But what I can tell you, with absolute certainty, is that you can find security in the embrace of your heavenly Father, of the God who first gave you life and continues to give it to you at every moment. He will be your firm support, but you will also realize that he fully respects your freedom.

114. In God's word, we find many expressions of his love. It is as if he tried to find different ways of showing that love, so that, with one of them at least, he could touch your heart. For example, there are times when God speaks of himself as an affectionate father who plays with his children: *"I led them with cords of compassion, with*

*bands of love. I was to them like those who lift infants to their cheeks"*
(Hos 11:4).

At other times, he speaks of himself as filled with the love of a mother whose visceral love for her children makes it impossible for her to neglect or abandon them: *"Can a woman forget her nursing child, or show no compassion for the child of her womb? Even these may forget, yet I will not forget you"* (Is 49:15).

He even compares himself to a lover who goes so far as to write his beloved on the palm of his hands, to keep her face always before him: *"See, I have inscribed you on the palms of my hands!"* (Is 49:6).

At other times, he emphasizes the strength and steadfastness of his invincible love: *"For the mountains may depart, and the hills be shaken, but my steadfast love shall not depart from you, and my covenant of peace shall not be shaken"* (Is 54:10).

Or he tells us that we have been awaited from eternity, for it was not by chance that we came into this world: *"I have loved you with an everlasting love; therefore I have continued my faithfulness to you"* (Jer 31:3).

Or he lets us know that he sees in us a beauty that no one else can see: *"For you are precious in my sight, and honored, and I love you"* (Is 43:4).

Or he makes us realize that his love is not cheerless, but pure joy, welling up whenever we allow ourselves to be loved by him: *"The Lord, your God, is in your midst, a warrior who gives victory. He will rejoice over you with gladness, he will renew you in his love; he will exult over you with loud singing"* (Zeph 3:17).

115. For him, you have worth; you are not insignificant. You are important to him, for you are the work of his hands. That is why he is concerned about you and looks to you with affection. "Trust the memory of God: his memory is not a 'hard disk' that 'saves' and 'archives' all our data. His memory is a heart filled with tender compassion, one that finds joy in 'deleting' from us every trace

of evil."[63] He does not keep track of your failings and he always helps you learn something even from your mistakes. Because he loves you. Try to keep still for a moment and let yourself feel his love. Try to silence all the noise within, and rest for a second in his loving embrace.

116. His is "a love that does not overwhelm or oppress, cast aside or reduce to silence, humiliate or domineer. It is the love of the Lord, a daily, discreet and respectful love; a love that is free and freeing, a love that heals and raises up. The love of the Lord has to do more with raising up than knocking down, with reconciling than forbidding, with offering new changes than condemning, with the future than the past."[64]

117. When he asks something of you, or simply makes you face life's challenges, he is hoping that you will make room for him to push you, to help you grow. He does not get upset if you share your questions with him. He is concerned when you *don't* talk to him, when you are not open to dialogue with him. The Bible tells us that Jacob fought with God (cf. Gen 32:25-31), but that did not keep him from persevering in his journey. The Lord himself urges us: "Come, let us argue it out" (Is 1:18). His love is so real, so true, so concrete, that it invites us to a relationship of openness and fruitful dialogue. Seek the closeness of our heavenly Father in the loving face of his courageous witnesses on earth!

# CHRIST SAVES YOU

118. The second great truth is that Christ, out of love, sacrificed himself completely in order to save you. His outstretched arms on the cross are the most telling sign that he is a friend who is willing

---

63  *Homily at Mass, XXXI World Youth Day in Krakow* (July 31, 2016): AAS 108 (2016), 963.

64  *Address at the Opening of the XXXIV World Youth Day in Panama* (January 24, 2019): *L'Osservatore Romano*, January 26, 2019, 12.

to stop at nothing: *"Having loved his own who were in the world, he loved them to the end"* (Jn 13:1).

St. Paul said that his life was one of complete trust in that self-sacrificing love: *"I now live by faith in the Son of God who loved me, and gave himself for me"* (Gal 2:20).

119. The same Christ who, by his cross, saved us from our sins, today continues to save and redeem us by the power of his total self-surrender. Look to his cross, cling to him, let him save you, for "those who accept his offer of salvation are set free from sin, sorrow, inner emptiness and loneliness."[65] And if you sin and stray far from him, he will come to lift you up by the power of his cross. Never forget that "he forgives us seventy times seven. Time and time again, he bears us on his shoulders. No one can strip us of the dignity bestowed upon us by this boundless and unfailing love. With a tenderness that never disappoints but is always capable of restoring our joy, he makes it possible for us to lift up our heads and to start anew."[66]

120. "We are saved by Jesus because he loves us and cannot go against his nature. We can do any number of things against him, yet he loves us and he saves us. For only what is loved can be saved. Only what is embraced can be transformed. The Lord's love is greater than all our problems, frailties and flaws. Yet it is precisely through our problems, frailties and flaws that he wants to write this love story. He embraced the prodigal son, he embraced Peter after his denials, and he always, always, always embraces us after every fall, helping us to rise and get back on our feet. Because the worst fall, and pay attention to this, *the worst fall, the one that can ruin our lives, is when we stay down and do not allow ourselves to be helped up.*"[67]

---

65  Apostolic Exhortation *Evangelii Gaudium* (November 24, 2013), no. 1: AAS 105 (2013), 1019.

66  Ibid., no. 3: AAS 105 (2013), 1020.

67  *Address at the Vigil with Young People, XXXIV World Youth Day in Panama* (January 26, 2019): *L'Osservatore Romano*, January 28-29, 2019, 6.

121. His forgiveness and salvation are not something we can buy, or that we have to acquire by our own works or efforts. He forgives us and sets us free without cost. His self-sacrifice on the cross is so great that we can never repay it, but only receive it with immense gratitude and with the joy of being more greatly loved than we could ever imagine: "He loved us first" (1 Jn 4:19).

122. Young people, beloved of the Lord, how valuable must you be if you were redeemed by the precious blood of Christ! Dear young people, "you are priceless! You are not up for sale! Please, do not let yourselves be bought. Do not let yourselves be seduced. Do not let yourselves be enslaved by forms of ideological colonization that put ideas in your heads, with the result that you end up becoming slaves, addicts, failures in life. You are priceless. You must repeat this always: I am not up for sale; I do not have a price. I am free! Fall in love with this freedom, which is what Jesus offers."[68]

123. Keep your eyes fixed on the outstretched arms of Christ crucified, let yourself be saved over and over again. And when you go to confess your sins, believe firmly in his mercy which frees you of your guilt. Contemplate his blood poured out with such great love, and let yourself be cleansed by it. In this way, you can be reborn ever anew.

## HE IS ALIVE!

124. Finally, there is a third truth, inseparable from the second: Christ is alive! We need to keep reminding ourselves of this, because we can risk seeing Jesus Christ simply as a fine model from the distant past, as a memory, as someone who saved us two thousand years ago. But that would be of no use to us: it would leave us unchanged, it would not set us free. The one who fills us with his grace, the one who liberates us, transforms us, heals and consoles us

---

68   *Address at the Meeting with Young People during the Synod* (October 6, 2018): *L'Osservatore Romano*, October 8-9, 2018, 7.

is someone fully alive. He is the Christ, risen from the dead, filled with supernatural life and energy, and robed in boundless light. That is why St. Paul could say: "If Christ has not been raised, your faith is futile" (1 Cor 15:7).

125. Alive, he can be present in your life at every moment, to fill it with light and to take away all sorrow and solitude. Even if all others depart, he will remain, as he promised: "I am with you always, to the end of the age" (Mt 28:20). He fills your life with his unseen presence; wherever you go, he will be waiting there for you. Because he did not only come in the past, but he comes to you today and every day, inviting you to set out toward ever new horizons.

126. See Jesus as happy, overflowing with joy. Rejoice with him as with a friend who has triumphed. They killed him, the holy one, the just one, the innocent one, but he triumphed in the end. Evil does not have the last word. Nor will it have the last word in your life, for you have a friend who loves you and wants to triumph in you. Your Savior lives.

127. Because he lives, there can be no doubt that goodness will have the upper hand in your life and that all our struggles will prove worthwhile. If this is the case, we can stop complaining and look to the future, for with him this is always possible. That is the certainty we have. Jesus is eternally alive. If we hold fast to him, we will have life, and be protected from the threats of death and violence that may assail us in life.

128. Every other solution will prove inadequate and temporary. It may be helpful for a time, but once again we will find ourselves exposed and abandoned before the storms of life. With Jesus, on the other hand, our hearts experience a security that is firmly rooted and enduring. St. Paul says that he wishes to be one with Christ in order "to know him and the power of his resurrection" (Phil 3:10).

That power will constantly be revealed in your lives too, for he came to give you life, "and life in abundance" (Jn 10:10).

129. If in your heart you can learn to appreciate the beauty of this message, if you are willing to encounter the Lord, if you are willing to let him love you and save you, if you can make friends with him and start to talk to him, the living Christ, about the realities of your life, then you will have a profound experience capable of sustaining your entire Christian life. You will also be able to share that experience with other young people. For "being a Christian is not the result of an ethical choice or a lofty idea, but the encounter with an event, a person, which gives life a new horizon and a decisive direction."[69]

# THE SPIRIT GIVES LIFE

130. In these three truths—God loves you; Christ is your Savior; he is alive—we see God the Father and Jesus. Wherever the Father and the Son are, there too is the Holy Spirit. He is the one who quietly opens hearts to receive that message. He keeps alive our hope of salvation, and he will help you grow in joy if you are open to his working. The Holy Spirit fills the heart of the risen Christ and then flows over into your lives. When you receive the Spirit, he draws you ever more deeply into the heart of Christ, so that you can grow in his love, his life and his power.

131. Ask the Holy Spirit each day to help you experience anew the great message. Why not? You have nothing to lose, and he can change your life, fill it with light and lead it along a better path. He takes nothing away from you, but instead helps you to find all that you need, and in the best possible way. Do you need love? You will not find it in dissipation, using other people, or trying to be possessive or domineering. You will find it in a way that will make

---

69   Benedict XVI, Encyclical Letter *Deus Caritas Est* (December 25, 2005), no. 1: *AAS* 98 (2006), 217.

you genuinely happy. Are you seeking powerful emotions? You will not experience them by accumulating material objects, spending money, chasing desperately after the things of this world. They will come, and in a much more beautiful and meaningful way, if you let yourself be prompted by the Holy Spirit.

132. Are you looking for passion? As that beautiful poem says: "Fall in love!" (or "let yourself be loved!"), because "nothing is more practical than finding God, than falling in love in a quite absolute, final way. What you are in love with, what seizes your imagination, will affect everything. It will decide what will get you out of bed in the morning, what you do with your evenings, how you spend your weekends, what you read, whom you know, what breaks your heart, and what amazes you with joy and gratitude. Fall in love, stay in love, and it will decide everything."[70] This love for God, that can approach everything in life with passion, is possible thanks to the Spirit, for "God's love has been poured into our hearts through the Holy Spirit who has been given to us" (Rom 5:5).

133. He is the source of youth at its best. For those who trust in the Lord are "like a tree planted by water sending out its roots by the stream; it shall not fear when heat comes, and its leaves shall stay green" (Jer 17:8). While "youths shall faint and be weary" (Is 40:30), those who wait for the Lord "shall renew their strength, they shall mount up with wings like eagles, they shall run and not be weary, they shall walk and not faint" (Is 40:31).

70   Pedro Arrupe, *Enamórate*.

# CHAPTER FIVE
# Paths of Youth

134. What does it mean to live the years of our youth in the transforming light of the Gospel? We need to raise this question, because youth, more than a source of pride, is a gift of God: "To be young is a grace, a blessing."[71] It is a gift that we can squander meaninglessly, or receive with gratitude and live to the full.

135. God is the giver of youth and he is at work in the life of each young person. Youth is a blessed time for the young and a grace for the Church and for the world. It is joy, a song of hope and a blessing. Making the most of our youthful years entails seeing this season of life as worthwhile in itself, and not simply as a brief prelude to adulthood.

## A TIME OF DREAMS AND DECISIONS

136. In Jesus' day, the passage from childhood was a significant step in life, one joyfully celebrated. When Jesus restored life to a man's daughter, he first called her a "child" (Mk 5:39), but then addressed her as a "young girl" (Mk 5:41). By saying to her: "Young girl, get up (*talitha cum*)," he made her more responsible for her life, opening before her the door to youth.

137. "Youth, as a phase in the development of the personality, is marked by dreams which gather momentum, by relationships which acquire more and more consistency and balance, by trials and experiments, and by choices which gradually build a life project. At this stage in life, the young are called to move forward

---

71  St. Paul VI, *Address for the Beatification of Nunzio Sulprizio* (December 1, 1963): AAS 56 (1964), 28.

without cutting themselves off from their roots, to build autonomy but not in solitude."[72]

138. The love of God and our relationship with the living Christ do not hold us back from dreaming; they do not require us to narrow our horizons. On the contrary, that love elevates us, encourages us and inspires us to a better and more beautiful life. Much of the longing present in the hearts of young people can be summed up in the word "restlessness." As St. Paul VI said, "In the very discontent that you often feel . . . a ray of light is present."[73] Restless discontent, combined with exhilaration before the opening up of new horizons, generates a boldness that leads you to stand up and take responsibility for a mission. This healthy restlessness typical of youth continues to dwell in every heart that remains young, open and generous. True inner peace coexists with that profound discontent. As St. Augustine said: "You have created us for yourself, Lord, and our hearts are restless until they find their rest in you."[74]

139. Sometime ago, a friend asked me what I see in a young person. My response was that "I see someone who is searching for his or her own path, who wants to fly on their two feet, who faces the world and looks at the horizon with eyes full of the future, full of hope as well as illusions. A young person stands on two feet as adults do, but unlike adults, whose feet are parallel, he always has one foot forward, ready to set out, to spring ahead. Always racing onward. To talk about young people is to talk about promise and to talk about joy. Young people have so much strength; they are able to look ahead with hope. A young person is a promise of life that implies a certain degree of tenacity. He is foolish enough to delude himself, and resilient enough to recover from that delusion."[75]

---

72  FD 65.

73  *Homily at Mass with Young People in Sydney* (December 2, 1970): AAS 63 (1971), 64.

74  *Confessions*, I, 1, 1: PL 32, 661.

75  *God Is Young. A Conversation with Thomas Leoncini*, New York, Random House, 2018, 4.

140. Some young people might hate this stage of life, because they want to continue being children or indefinitely prolong their adolescence and put off having to make decisions. "Fear of the definitive thus generates a kind of paralysis of decision-making. Yet youth cannot remain on hold. It is the age of choices and herein lies its fascination and its greatest responsibility. Young people make decisions in professional, social and political fields, and in other more radical ways that determine the shape of their lives."[76] They also make decisions about love, choosing a spouse and starting a family. We will look at these issues more closely in the final chapters, when dealing with individual vocations and their discernment.

141. But opposed to these hopes and dreams that generate decisions, there is always the temptation to complain or give up. "We can leave that to those who worship the 'goddess of lament' . . . She is a false goddess: she makes you take the wrong road. When everything seems to be standing still and stagnant, when our personal issues trouble us, and social problems do not meet with the right responses, it does no good to give up. Jesus is the way: welcome him into your 'boat' and put out into the deep! He is the Lord! He changes the way we see life. Faith in Jesus leads to greater hope, to a certainty based not on our qualities and skills, but on the word of God, on the invitation that comes from him. Without making too many human calculations, and without worrying about things that challenge your security, put out into the deep. Go out of yourselves."[77]

142. Keep following your hopes and dreams. But be careful about one temptation that can hold us back. It is anxiety. Anxiety can work against us by making us give up whenever we do not see instant results. Our best dreams are only attained through hope, patience and commitment, and not in haste. At the same time, we

---

76   FD, no. 68.

77   *Meeting with Young People in Cagliari* (September 22, 2013): AAS 105 (2013), 904-905.

should not be hesitant, afraid to take chances or make mistakes. Avoid the paralysis of the living dead, who have no life because they are afraid to take risks, to make mistakes or to persevere in their commitments. Even if you make mistakes, you can always get up and start over, for no one has the right to rob you of hope.

143. Dear young people, make the most of these years of your youth. Don't observe life from a balcony. Don't confuse happiness with an armchair, or live your life behind a screen. Whatever you do, do not become the sorry sight of an abandoned vehicle! Don't be parked cars, but dream freely and make good decisions. Take risks, even if it means making mistakes. Don't go through life anaesthetized or approach the world like tourists. Make a ruckus! Cast out the fears that paralyze you, so that you don't become young mummies. Live! Give yourselves over to the best of life! Open the door of the cage, go out and fly! Please, don't take early retirement.

## A THIRST FOR LIFE AND EXPERIENCE

144. While drawn toward the future and its promise, young people also have a powerful desire to experience the present moment, to make the most of the opportunities life offers. Our world is filled with beauty! How can we look down upon God's many gifts?

145. Contrary to what many people think, the Lord does not want to stifle these desires for a fulfilling life. We do well to remember the words of an Old Testament sage: "My child, treat yourself well, according to your means, and present your offerings to the Lord; do not deprive yourself of a day's enjoyment, do not let your share of desired good pass by" (Sir 14:11, 14). The true God, who loves you, wants you to be happy. For this reason, the Bible also contains this piece of advice to young people: "Rejoice, young man, while you are young, and let your heart cheer you in the days of your youth . . . banish anxiety from your mind" (Ec 11:9-10).

For God "richly provides us with everything for our enjoyment" (1 Tim 6:17).

146. How could God take pleasure in someone incapable of enjoying his small everyday blessings, someone blind to the simple pleasures we find all around us? "No one is worse than one who is grudging to himself" (Sir 14:6). Far from obsessively seeking new pleasures, which would keep us from making the most of the present moment, we are asked to open our eyes and take a moment to experience fully and with gratitude every one of life's little gifts.

147. Clearly, God's word asks you to enjoy the present, not simply to prepare for the future: "Do not worry about tomorrow, for tomorrow will bring worries of its own; today's trouble is enough for today" (Mt 6:34). But this is not the same as embarking irresponsibly on a life of dissipation that can only leave us empty and perpetually dissatisfied. Rather, it is about living the present to the full, spending our energies on good things, cultivating fraternity, following Jesus and making the most of life's little joys as gifts of God's love.

148. Cardinal Francis Xavier Nguyên Van Thuân, when imprisoned in a concentration camp, refused to do nothing but await the day when he would be set free. He chose "to live the present moment, filling it to the brim with love." He decided: "I will seize the occasions that present themselves every day; I will accomplish ordinary actions in an extraordinary way."[78] As you work to achieve your dreams, make the most of each day and do your best to let each moment brim with love. This youthful day may well be your last, and so it is worth the effort to live it as enthusiastically and fully as possible.

149. This can also be applied to times of difficulty, that have to be fully experienced if we are to learn the message they can teach us.

---

78  *Five Loaves and Two Fish*, Pauline Books and Media, 2003, 9, 13.

In the words of the Swiss Bishops: "God is there where we thought he had abandoned us and there was no further hope of salvation. It is a paradox, but for many Christians, suffering and darkness have become . . . places of encounter with God."[79] The desire to live fully and experience new things is also felt by many young people with physical, mental and sensory disabilities. Even though they may not always be able to have the same experiences as others, they possess amazing resources and abilities that are often far above average. The Lord Jesus grants them other gifts, which the community is called to recognize and appreciate, so that they can discover his plan of love for each of them.

## IN FRIENDSHIP WITH CHRIST

150. No matter how much you live the experience of these years of your youth, you will never know their deepest and fullest meaning unless you encounter each day your best friend, the friend who is Jesus.

151. Friendship is one of life's gifts and a grace from God. Through our friends, the Lord refines us and leads us to maturity. Faithful friends, who stand at our side in times of difficulty, are also a reflection of the Lord's love, his gentle and consoling presence in our lives. The experience of friendship teaches us to be open, understanding and caring toward others, to come out of our own comfortable isolation and to share our lives with others. For this reason, "there is nothing so precious as a faithful friend" (Sir 6:15).

152. Friendship is no fleeting or temporary relationship, but one that is stable, firm and faithful, and matures with the passage of time. A relationship of affection that brings us together and a generous love that makes us seek the good of our friend. Friends may

---

79  Conférence des Évêques Suisses, *Prendre le temps: pour toi, pour moi, pour nous*, February 2, 2018.

be quite different from one another, but they always have things in common that draw them closer in mutual openness and trust.[80]

153. Friendship is so important that Jesus calls himself a friend: "I do not call you servants any longer, but I call you friends" (Jn 15:15). By the gift of his grace, we are elevated in such a way that we truly become his friends. With the same love that Christ pours out on us, we can love him in turn and share his love with others, in the hope that they too will take their place in the community of friendship he established. And even as he enjoys the complete bliss of the life of the resurrection, we, for our part, can work generously to help him build his kingdom in this world, by bringing his message, his light, and above all his love, to others (cf. Jn 15:16). The disciples heard Jesus calling them to be his friends. It was an invitation that did not pressure them, but gently appealed to their freedom. "Come and see," Jesus told them; so "they came and saw where he was staying, and they remained with him that day" (Jn 1:39). After that unexpected and moving encounter, they left everything and followed him.

154. Friendship with Jesus cannot be broken. He never leaves us, even though at times it appears that he keeps silent. When we need him, he makes himself known to us (cf. Jer 29:14); he remains at our side wherever we go (cf. Jos 1:9). He never breaks his covenant. He simply asks that we not abandon him: "Abide in me" (Jn 15:4). But even if we stray from him, "he remains faithful, for he cannot deny himself" (2 Tim 2:13).

155. With a friend, we can speak and share our deepest secrets. With Jesus too, we can always have a conversation. Prayer is both a challenge and an adventure. And what an adventure it is! Gradually Jesus makes us appreciate his grandeur and draw nearer to him. Prayer enables us to share with him every aspect of our lives and to rest confidently in his embrace. At the same time, it gives

---

80   Cf. St. Thomas Aquinas, *Summa Theologiae*, II-II, q. 23, art. 1.

us a share in his own life and love. When we pray, "we open every-thing we do" to him, and we give him room "so that he can act, enter and claim victory."[81]

156. In this way, we can experience a constant closeness to him, greater than anything we can experience with another person: "It is no longer I who live, but it is Christ who lives in me" (Gal 2:20). Do not deprive your youth of this friendship. You will be able to feel him at your side not only when you pray, but at every moment. Try to look for him, and you will have the beautiful experience of seeing that he is always at your side. That is what the disciples of Emmaus experienced when, as they walked along dejectedly, Jesus "drew near and walked with them" (Lk 24:15). In the words of a saint, "Christianity is not a collection of truths to be believed, rules to be followed, or prohibitions. Seen that way, it puts us off. Christianity is a person who loved me immensely, who demands and asks for my love. Christianity is Christ."[82]

157. Jesus can bring all the young people of the Church together in a single dream, "a great dream, a dream with a place for everyone. The dream for which Jesus gave his life on the cross, for which the Holy Spirit was poured out on the day of Pentecost and brought fire to the heart of every man and woman, to your heart and mine. To your heart too, he brought that fire, in the hope of finding room for it to grow and flourish. A dream whose name is Jesus, planted by the Father in the confidence that it would grow and live in every heart. A concrete dream who is a person, running through our veins, thrilling our hearts and making them dance."[83]

---

81  *Address to the Volunteers of the XXXIV World Youth Day in Panama* (January 27, 2019): *L'Osservatore Romano*, January 28-29, 2019, 11.

82  St. Oscar Romero, *Homily* (November 6, 1977), in *Su Pensamiento*, I-II, San Salvador, 2000, 312.

83  *Address at the Opening of the XXXIV World Youth Day in Panama* (January 24, 2019): *L'Osservatore Romano*, January 26, 2019, 12.

# GROWTH IN MATURITY

158. Many young people are concerned about their bodies, trying to build up physical strength or improve their appearance. Others work to develop their talents and knowledge, so as to feel more sure of themselves. Some aim higher, seeking to become more involved and to grow spiritually. St. John said: "I write to you, young people, because you are strong and the word of God abides in you" (1 Jn 2:14). Seeking the Lord, keeping his word, entrusting our life to him and growing in the virtues: all these things make young hearts strong. That is why you need to stay connected to Jesus, to "remain online" with him, since you will not grow happy and holy by your own efforts and intelligence alone. Just as you try not to lose your connection to the internet, make sure that you stay connected to the Lord. That means not cutting off dialogue, listening to him, sharing your life with him and, whenever you aren't sure what you should do, asking him: "Jesus, what would you do in my place?"[84]

159. I hope that you will be serious enough about yourselves to make an effort to grow spiritually. Along with all the other exciting things about youth, there is also the beauty of seeking "righteousness, faith, love and peace" (2 Tim 2:22). This does not involve losing anything of your spontaneity, boldness, enthusiasm and tenderness. Becoming an adult does not mean you have to abandon what is best about this stage of your lives. If you do, the Lord may one day reproach you: "I remember the devotion of your youth, your love as a bride, and how you followed me in the wilderness" (Jer 2:2).

160. Adults, too, have to mature without losing the values of youth. Every stage of life is a permanent grace, with its own enduring value. The experience of a youth well lived always remains in our heart. It continues to grow and bear fruit throughout adulthood. Young people are naturally attracted by an infinite horizon opening

---

84   Cf. *Meeting with Young People in the National Shrine of Maipú*, Santiago de Chile (January 17, 2018): *L'Osservatore Romano*, January 19, 2018, 7.

up before them.[85] Adult life, with its securities and comforts, can risk shrinking that horizon and losing that youthful excitement. The very opposite should happen: as we mature, grow older and structure our lives, we should never lose that enthusiasm and openness to an ever greater reality. At every moment in life, we can renew our youthfulness. When I began my ministry as Pope, the Lord broadened my horizons and granted me renewed youth. The same thing can happen to a couple married for many years, or to a monk in his monastery. There are things we need to "let go of" as the years pass, but growth in maturity can coexist with a fire constantly rekindled, with a heart ever young.

161. Growing older means preserving and cherishing the most precious things about our youth, but it also involves having to purify those things that are not good and receiving new gifts from God so we can develop the things that really matter. At times, a certain inferiority complex can make you overlook your flaws and weaknesses, but that can hold you back from growth in maturity. Instead, let yourself be loved by God, for he loves you just as you are. He values and respects you, but he also keeps offering you more: more of his friendship, more fervor in prayer, more hunger for his word, more longing to receive Christ in the Eucharist, more desire to live by his Gospel, more inner strength, more peace and spiritual joy.

162. But I would also remind you that you won't become holy and find fulfillment by copying others. Imitating the Saints does not mean copying their lifestyle and their way of living holiness: "there are some testimonies that may prove helpful and inspiring, but that we are not meant to copy, for that could even lead us astray from the one specific path that the Lord has in mind for us."[86] You have to discover who you are and develop your own way of being holy, whatever others may say or think. Becoming a saint means

---

85   Cf. Romano Guardini, *Die Lebensalter. Ihre ethische und pädagogische Bedeutung*, Würzburg, 3rd ed., 1955, 20.

86   Apostolic Exhortation *Gaudete et Exsultate* (March 19, 2018), no. 11.

becoming more fully yourself, becoming what the Lord wished to dream and create, and not a photocopy. Your life ought to be a prophetic stimulus to others and leave a mark on this world, the unique mark that only you can leave. Whereas if you simply copy someone else, you will deprive this earth, and heaven too, of something that no one else can offer. I think of St. John of the Cross, who wrote in his *Spiritual Canticle* that everyone should benefit from his spiritual advice "in his or her own way,"[87] for the one God wishes to manifest his grace "to some in one way and to others in another."[88]

# PATHS OF FRATERNITY

163. Your spiritual growth is expressed above all by your growth in fraternal, generous and merciful love. St. Paul prayed: "May the Lord make you increase and abound in love for one another and for all" (1 Thes 3:12). How wonderful it would be to experience this "ecstasy" of coming out of ourselves and seeking the good of others, even to the sacrifice of our lives.

164. When an encounter with God is called an "ecstasy," it is because it takes us out of ourselves, lifts us up and overwhelms us with God's love and beauty. Yet we can also experience ecstasy when we recognize in others their hidden beauty, their dignity and their grandeur as images of God and children of the Father. The Holy Spirit wants to make us come out of ourselves, to embrace others with love and to seek their good. That is why it is always better to live the faith together and to show our love by living in community and sharing with other young people our affection, our time, our faith and our troubles. The Church offers many different possibilities for living our faith in community, for everything is easier when we do it together.

---

87  *Spiritual Canticle*, Red. B, Prologue, 2.
88  Ibid., XIV-XV, 2.

165. Hurts you have experienced might tempt you to withdraw from others, to turn in on yourself and to nurse feelings of anger, but never stop listening to God's call to forgiveness. The Bishops of Rwanda put it well: "In order to reconcile with another person, you must first of all be able to see the goodness in that person, the goodness God created him with . . . This requires great effort to distinguish the offence from the offender; it means you hate the offence the person has committed, but you love the person despite his weakness, because in him you see the image of God."[89]

166. There are times when all our youthful energy, dreams and enthusiasm can flag because we are tempted to dwell on ourselves and our problems, our hurt feelings and our grievances. Don't let this happen to you! You will grow old before your time. Each age has its beauty, and the years of our youth need to be marked by shared ideals, hopes and dreams, great horizons that we can contemplate together.

167. God loves the joy of young people. He wants them especially to share in the joy of fraternal communion, the sublime joy felt by those who share with others, for "it is more blessed to give than to receive" (Acts 20:35). "God loves a cheerful giver" (2 Cor 9:7). Fraternal love multiplies our ability to experience joy, since it makes us rejoice in the good of others: "Rejoice with those who rejoice, weep with those who weep" (Rom 12:15). May your youthful spontaneity increasingly find expression in fraternal love and a constant readiness to forgive, to be generous, and to build community. As an African proverb says: "If you want to go fast, go alone. If you want to go far, go together." Let us not allow ourselves to be robbed of fraternity.

---

89    Episcopal Conference of Rwanda, *Letter of the Catholic Bishops of Rwanda for Christians in the Extraordinary Year of Reconciliation*, Kigali (January 18, 2018), 17.

# YOUNG AND COMMITTED

168. At times, seeing a world so full of violence and selfishness, young people can be tempted to withdraw into small groups, shunning the challenges and issues posed by life in society and in the larger world. They may feel that they are experiencing fraternity and love, but their small group may in fact become nothing other than an extension of their own ego. This is even more serious if they think of the lay vocation simply as a form of service inside the Church: serving as lectors, acolytes, catechists, and so forth. They forget that the lay vocation is directed above all to charity within the family and to social and political charity. It is a concrete and faith-based commitment to the building of a new society. It involves living in the midst of society and the world in order to bring the Gospel everywhere, to work for the growth of peace, harmony, justice, human rights and mercy, and thus for the extension of God's kingdom in this world.

169. I ask young people to go beyond their small groups and to build "social friendship, where everyone works for the common good. Social enmity, on the other hand, is destructive. Families are destroyed by enmity. Countries are destroyed by enmity. The world is destroyed by enmity. And the greatest enmity of all is war. Today we see that the world is destroying itself by war . . . So find ways of building social friendship."[90] It is not easy, it always means having to give something up and to negotiate, but if we do it for the sake of helping others, we can have the magnificent experience of setting our differences aside and working together for something greater. If, as a result of our own simple and at times costly efforts, we can find points of agreement amid conflict, build bridges and make peace for the benefit of all, then we will experience the miracle of the culture of encounter. This is something which young people can dare to pursue with passion.

---

90  *Greeting to Young People of the Father Félix Varela Cultural Centre in Havana* (September 20, 2015): *L'Osservatore Romano*, September 21-22, 2015, 6.

170. The Synod recognized that "albeit in a different way from earlier generations, social commitment is a specific feature of today's young people. Alongside some who are indifferent, there are many others who are ready to commit themselves to initiatives of volunteer work, active citizenship and social solidarity. They need to be accompanied and encouraged to use their talents and skills creatively, and to be encouraged to take up their responsibilities. Social engagement and direct contact with the poor remain fundamental ways of finding or deepening one's faith and the discernment of one's vocation . . . It was also noted that the young are prepared to enter political life so as to build the common good."[91]

171. Today, thank God, many young people in parishes, schools, movements and university groups often go out to spend time with the elderly and the infirm, or to visit poor neighborhoods, or to meet people's needs through "nights of charity." Very often, they come to realize that there they receive much more than what they give. We grow in wisdom and maturity when we take the time to touch the suffering of others. The poor have a hidden wisdom and, with a few simple words, they can help us discover unexpected values.

172. Other young people take part in social programs that build houses for the homeless, or reclaim contaminated areas or offer various kinds of assistance to the needy. It would be helpful if this shared energy could be channelled and organized in a more stable way and with clear goals, so as to be even more effective. University students can apply their knowledge in an interdisciplinary way, together with young people of other churches or religions, in order to propose solutions to social problems.

173. As in the miracle of Jesus, the bread and the fish provided by young people can multiply (cf. Jn 6:4-13). As in the parable, the small seeds sown by young people can yield a rich harvest (cf. Mt 13:23, 31-32). All of this has its living source in the Eucharist, in

---

91   FD, no. 46.

which our bread and our wine are transformed to grant us eternal life. Young people face immense and difficult challenges. With faith in the risen Lord, they can confront them with creativity and hope, ever ready to be of service, like the servants at the wedding feast, who unknowingly cooperated in Jesus' first miracle. They did nothing more than follow the order of his Mother: "Do whatever he tells you" (Jn 2:5). Mercy, creativity and hope make life grow.

174. I want to encourage all of you in this effort, because I know that "your young hearts want to build a better world. I have been following news reports of the many young people throughout the world who have taken to the streets to express the desire for a more just and fraternal society. Young people taking to the streets! The young want to be protagonists of change. Please, do not leave it to others to be protagonists of change. You are the ones who hold the future! Through you, the future enters into the world. I ask you also to be protagonists of this transformation. You are the ones who hold the key to the future! Continue to fight apathy and to offer a Christian response to the social and political troubles emerging in different parts of the world. I ask you to build the future, to work for a better world. Dear young people, please, do not be bystanders in life. Get involved! Jesus was not a bystander. He got involved. Don't stand aloof, but immerse yourselves in the reality of life, as Jesus did."[92] Above all, in one way or another, fight for the common good, serve the poor, be protagonists of the revolution of charity and service, capable of resisting the pathologies of consumerism and superficial individualism.

## COURAGEOUS MISSIONARIES

175. Filled with the love of Christ, young people are called to be witnesses of the Gospel wherever they find themselves, by the way they live. St. Alberto Hurtado once said that "being an apostle

---

92   *Address at the Vigil, XXVIII World Youth Day in Rio de Janeiro* (July 27, 2013): AAS 105 (2013), 663.

does not mean wearing a lapel pin; it is not about speaking about the truth but living it, embodying it, being transformed in Christ. Being an apostle does not mean carrying a torch in hand, possessing the light, but being that light . . . The Gospel, more than a lesson, is an example. A message that becomes a life fully lived."[93]

176. The importance of witness does not mean that we should be silent about the word. Why should we not speak of Jesus, why should we not tell others that he gives us strength in life, that we enjoy talking with him, that we benefit from meditating on his words? Young people, do not let the world draw you only into things that are wrong and superficial. Learn to swim against the tide, learn how to share Jesus and the faith he has given you. May you be moved by that same irresistible impulse that led St. Paul to say: "Woe to me if I do not proclaim the Gospel" (1 Cor 9:16)!

177. "Where does Jesus send us? There are no borders, no limits: he sends us everywhere. The Gospel is for everyone, not just for some. It is not only for those who seem closer to us, more receptive, more welcoming. It is for everyone. Do not be afraid to go and bring Christ into every area of life, to the fringes of society, even to those who seem farthest away and most indifferent. The Lord seeks all; he wants everyone to feel the warmth of his mercy and his love."[94] He invites us to be fearless missionaries wherever we are and in whatever company we find ourselves: in our neighborhoods, in school or sports or social life, in volunteer service or in the workplace. Wherever we are, we always have an opportunity to share the joy of the Gospel. That is how the Lord goes out to meet everyone. He loves you, dear young people, for you are the means by which he can spread his light and hope. He is counting on your courage, your boldness and your enthusiasm.

---

93  *Ustedes son la luz del mundo.* Address in Cerro San Cristóbal, Chile, 1940. The text can be found at: *https://www.padrealbertohurtado.cl/escritos-2/.*

94  *Homily at Mass, XXVIII World Youth Day in Rio de Janeiro* (July 28, 2013): AAS 105 (2013), 665.

178. Don't think that this mission is soft and easy. Some young people have given their lives for the sake of missionary outreach. As the Korean bishops put it: "we hope that we can be grains of wheat and instruments for the salvation of humanity, following upon the example of the martyrs. Though our faith is as small as a mustard seed, God will give it growth and use it as an instrument for his work of salvation."[95] Young friends, don't wait until tomorrow to contribute your energy, your audacity and your creativity to changing our world. Your youth is not an "in-between time." You are the *now* of God, and he wants you to bear fruit.[96] For "it is in giving that we receive."[97] The best way to prepare a bright future is to experience the present as best we can, with commitment and generosity.

95 Catholic Bishops' Conference of Korea, *Pastoral Letter on the occasion of the 150th Anniversary of the Martyrdom during the Byeong-in Persecution* (March 30, 2016).

96 Cf. *Homily at Mass, XXXIV World Youth Day in Panama* (January 27, 2018): *L'Osservatore Romano*, January 28-29, 2019, 12.

97 "Lord, make me a channel of your peace," prayer inspired by St. Francis of Assisi.

# CHAPTER SIX
# Young People with Roots

179. I have sometimes seen young and beautiful trees, their branches reaching to the sky, pushing ever higher, and they seemed a song of hope. Later, following a storm, I would find them fallen and lifeless. They lacked deep roots. They spread their branches without being firmly planted, and so they fell as soon as nature unleashed her power. That is why it pains me to see young people sometimes being encouraged to build a future without roots, as if the world were just starting now. For "it is impossible for us to grow unless we have strong roots to support us and to keep us firmly grounded. It is easy to drift off, when there is nothing to clutch onto, to hold onto."[98]

## DON'T ALLOW YOURSELVES TO BE UPROOTED

180. This is an important issue, and I want to spend a brief chapter discussing it. If we appreciate this issue, we can distinguish the joy of youth from a false cult of youth that can be used to seduce and manipulate young people.

181. Think about it: if someone tells young people to ignore their history, to reject the experiences of their elders, to look down on the past and to look forward to a future that he holds out, doesn't it then become easy to draw them along so that they only do what he tells them? He needs the young to be shallow, uprooted and distrustful, so that they can trust only in his promises and act according to his plans. That is how various ideologies operate: they destroy (or deconstruct) all differences so that they can reign unopposed. To do so, however, they need young people who have no

---

98    *Address at the Vigil, XXIV World Youth Day in Panama*, (January 26, 2019): *L'Osservatore Romano*, January 28-29, 2019, 6.

use for history, who spurn the spiritual and human riches inherited from past generations, and are ignorant of everything that came before them.

182. These masters of manipulation also use another tactic: the cult of youth, which dismisses all that is not young as contemptible and outmoded. The youthful body becomes the symbol of this new cult; everything associated with that body is idolized and lusted after, while whatever is not young is despised. But this cult of youth is simply an expedient that ultimately proves degrading to the young; it strips them of any real value and uses them for personal, financial or political profit.

183. Dear young friends, do not let them exploit your youth to promote a shallow life that confuses beauty with appearances. Realize that there is beauty in the laborer who returns home grimy and unkempt, but with the joy of having earned food for his family. There is extraordinary beauty in the fellowship of a family at table, generously sharing what food it has. There is beauty in the wife, slightly dishevelled and no longer young, who continues to care for her sick husband despite her own failing health. Long after the springtime of their courtship has passed, there is beauty in the fidelity of those couples who still love one another in the autumn of life, those elderly people who still hold hands as they walk. There is also a beauty, unrelated to appearances or fashionable dress, in all those men and women who pursue their personal vocation with love, in selfless service of community or nation, in the hard work of building a happy family, in the selfless and demanding effort to advance social harmony. To find, to disclose and to highlight this beauty, which is like that of Christ on the cross, is to lay the foundations of genuine social solidarity and the culture of encounter.

184. Along with the stratagems of a false cult of youth and appearance, we are also witnessing attempts to promote a spirituality without God, an affectivity without community or concern for those

who suffer, a fear of the poor, viewed as dangerous, and a variety of claims to offer a future paradise that nonetheless seems increasingly distant. I do not want to offer you any such thing, and with great love I urge you not to let yourselves be taken in by this ideology. It will not make you any younger, but enslave you instead. I propose another way, one born of freedom, enthusiasm, creativity and new horizons, while at the same time cultivating the roots that nourish and sustain us.

185. In this regard, I would note that "many Synod Fathers coming from non-Western contexts pointed out that in their countries globalization is bringing with it forms of cultural colonization that sever young people from their cultural and religious roots. The Church needs to make a commitment to accompanying these young people, so that in the process they do not lose sight of the most precious features of their identity."[99]

186. Today, in fact, we see a tendency to "homogenize" young people, blurring what is distinctive about their origins and backgrounds, and turning them into a new line of malleable goods. This produces a cultural devastation that is just as serious as the disappearance of species of animals and plants.[100] For this reason, in addressing young indigenous people gathered in Panama, I encouraged them to "care for your roots, because from the roots comes the strength that is going to make you grow, flourish and bear fruit."[101]

## YOUR RELATIONSHIP WITH THE ELDERLY

187. At the Synod, we heard that "the young are focused on the future and they face life with energy and dynamism. But they are also tempted . . . to give little attention to the memory of the past

---

99   FD, no. 14.

100   Cf. Encyclical Letter *Laudato Si'* (May 24, 2015), 145: AAS 107 (2015), 906.

101   *Video Messsage for the World Meeting of Indigenous Youth in Panama* (January 17-21, 2019): *L'Osservatore Romano*, January 19, 2019, 8.

from which they come, in particular the many gifts transmitted to them by their parents, their grandparents and the cultural experience of the society in which they live. Helping the young to discover the living richness of the past, to treasure its memory and to make use of it for their choices and opportunities, is a genuine act of love toward them, for the sake of their growth and the decisions they are called to make."[102]

188. The word of God encourages us to remain close to the elderly, so that we can benefit from their experience: "Stand in the assembly of the elders. Who is wise? Cling to him . . . If you see an intelligent man, visit him; let your foot wear out his doorstep" (Sir 6:34, 36). In every case, the long years they lived and all they have experienced in life should make us look to them with respect: "You shall rise up before the hoary head" (Lev 19:32). For "the glory of young men is their strength, but the beauty of old men is their grey hair" (Prov 20:29).

189. The Bible also tells us: "Listen to your father who begot you, and do not despise your mother when she is old" (Prov 23:22). The command to honor our father and mother "is the first commandment to carry a promise with it" (Eph 6:2, cf. Ex 20:12; Deut 5:16; Lev 19:3), and that promise is: "that it may be well with you and that you may live long on the earth" (Eph 6:3).

190. This does not mean having to agree with everything adults say or approving all their actions. A young person should always have a critical spirit. St. Basil the Great encouraged the young to esteem the classical Greek authors, but to accept only whatever good they could teach.[103] It is really a matter of being open to receiving a wisdom passed down from generation to generation, a wisdom familiar with human weakness and not deserving to vanish before the novelties of the consumer society and the market.

102  FD, no. 35.

103  Cf. Ad Adolescentes, I, 2: PG 31, 565.

191. The world has never benefited, nor will it ever benefit, from a rupture between generations. That is the siren song of a future without roots and origins. It is the lie that would have you believe that only what is new is good and beautiful. When intergenerational relationships exist, a collective memory is present in communities, as each generation takes up the teachings of its predecessors and in turn bequeaths a legacy to its successors. In this way, they provide frames of reference for firmly establishing a new society. As the old saying goes: "If the young had knowledge and the old strength, there would be nothing they could not accomplish."

## DREAMS AND VISIONS

192. The prophecy of Joel contains a verse that expresses this nicely: "I will pour out my Spirit upon all flesh, and your sons and your daughters shall prophesy, and your young men shall see visions, and your old men shall dream dreams" (3:1; cf. Acts 2:17). When young and old alike are open to the Holy Spirit, they make a wonderful combination. The old dream dreams, and the young see visions. How do the two complement one another?

193. The elderly have dreams built up of memories and images that bear the mark of their long experience. If young people sink roots in those dreams, they can peer into the future; they can have visions that broaden their horizons and show them new paths. But if the elderly do not dream, young people lose clear sight of the horizon.

194. Perhaps our parents have preserved a memory that can help us imagine the dream our grandparents dreamed for us. All of us, even before our birth, received, as a blessing from our grandparents, a dream filled with love and hope, the dream of a better life. Even if not our grandparents, surely some of our great-grandparents had that happy dream as they contemplated their children and then grandchildren in the cradle. The very first dream of all is the creative dream of God our Father, which precedes and accompanies

the lives of all his children. The memory of this blessing that extends from generation to generation is a precious legacy that we should keep alive so that we too can pass it on.

195. That is why it is a good thing to let older people tell their long stories, which sometimes seem legendary or fanciful—they are the dreams of old people—yet are often full of rich experiences, of eloquent symbols, of hidden messages. These stories take time to tell, and we should be prepared to listen patiently and let them sink in, even though they are much longer than what we are used to in social media. We have to realize that the wisdom needed for life bursts the confines of our present-day media resources.

196. In the book *Sharing the Wisdom of Time*,[104] I expressed some thoughts in the form of questions. "What do I ask of the elders among whom I count myself? I call us to be memory keepers. We grandfathers and grandmothers need to form a choir. I envision elders as a permanent choir of a great spiritual sanctuary, where prayers of supplication and songs of praise support the larger community that works and struggles in the field of life."[105] It is a beautiful thing when "young men and maidens together, old men and children, praise the name of the Lord" (Ps 148:12-13).

197. What can we elderly persons give to the young? "We can remind today's young people, who have their own blend of heroic ambitions and insecurities, that a life without love is an arid life."[106] What can we tell them? "We can tell fearful young people that anxiety about the future can be overcome."[107] What can we teach them? "We can teach those young people, sometimes so focused on

---

104 Cf. Pope Francis and Friends, *Sharing the Wisdom of Time*, Chicago, Loyola Press, 2018.

105 Ibid., 12.

106 Ibid., 13.

107 Ibid.

themselves, that there is more joy in giving than in receiving, and that love is not only shown in words, but also in actions."[108]

## TAKING RISKS TOGETHER

198. A love that is generous and outgoing, that acts and takes risks, may at times make mistakes. Here we may find timely the witness of Maria Gabriella Perin, who lost her father shortly after her birth: she reflects on how this influenced her life, in a relationship that did not last but that left her a mother and now a grandmother. "What I know is that God makes stories. In his genius and mercy, he takes our triumphs and our failures and weaves beautiful tapestries that are full of irony. The reverse of the fabric may look messy with its tangled threads—the events of our life—and maybe this is the side we dwell on when we doubt. But the right side of the tapestry displays a magnificent story, and this is the side that God sees."[109] When older people look at life closely, often they instinctively know what lies behind the tangled threads, and they recognize what God can create even out of our mistakes.

199. If we journey together, young and old, we can be firmly rooted in the present, and from here, revisit the past and look to the future. To revisit the past in order to learn from history and heal old wounds that at times still trouble us. To look to the future in order to nourish our enthusiasm, cause dreams to emerge, awaken prophecies and enable hope to blossom. Together, we can learn from one another, warm hearts, inspire minds with the light of the Gospel, and lend new strength to our hands.

200. Roots are not anchors chaining us to past times and preventing us from facing the present and creating something new. Instead, they are a fixed point from which we can grow and meet new challenges. It does us no good "to sit down and long for times past; we

108 Ibid.
109 Ibid., 162-163.

must meet our culture with realism and love and fill it with the Gospel. We are sent today to proclaim the Good News of Jesus to a new age. We need to love this time with all its opportunities and risks, its joys and sorrows, its riches and its limits, its successes and failures."[110]

201. During the Synod, one of the young auditors from the Samoan Islands spoke of the Church as a canoe, in which the elderly help to keep on course by judging the position of the stars, while the young keep rowing, imagining what waits for them ahead. Let us steer clear of young people who think that adults represent a meaning-less past, and those adults who always think they know how young people should act. Instead, let us all climb aboard the same canoe and together seek a better world, with the constantly renewed momentum of the Holy Spirit.

---

110 Eduardo Pironio, *Message to Young Argentinians at the National Youth Meeting in Cordoba*, (September 12-15, 1985), 2.

# CHAPTER SEVEN

# Youth Ministry

202. Youth ministry, as traditionally carried out, has been significantly affected by social and cultural changes. Young people frequently fail to find in our usual programs a response to their concerns, their needs, their problems and issues. The proliferation and growth of groups and movements predominantly associated with the young can be considered the work of the Holy Spirit who constantly shows us new paths. Even so, there is a need to look at the ways such groups participate in the Church's overall pastoral care, as well as a need for greater communion among them and a better coordination of their activities. Although it is never easy to approach young people, two things have become increasingly evident: the realization that the entire community has to be involved in evangelizing them, and the urgent requirement that young people take on a greater role in pastoral outreach.

## A PASTORAL CARE THAT IS SYNODAL

203. I want to state clearly that young people themselves are agents of youth ministry. Certainly they need to he helped and guided, but at the same time left free to develop new approaches, with creativity and a certain audacity. So I will not attempt here to propose a kind of manual of youth ministry or a practical pastoral guide. I am more concerned with helping young people to use their insight, ingenuity and knowledge to address the issues and concerns of other young people in their own language.

204. The young make us see the need for new styles and new strategies. For example, while adults often worry about having everything properly planned, with regular meetings and fixed times, most young people today have little interest in this kind of pastoral

approach. Youth ministry needs to become more flexible: inviting young people to events or occasions that provide an opportunity not only for learning, but also for conversing, celebrating, singing, listening to real stories and experiencing a shared encounter with the living God.

205. At the same time, we should take into greater consideration those practices that have shown their value—the methods, language and aims that have proved truly effective in bringing young people to Christ and the Church. It does not matter where they are coming from or what labels they have received, whether "conservative" or "liberal," "traditional" or "progressive." What is important is that we make use of everything that has borne good fruit and effectively communicates the joy of the Gospel.

206. Youth ministry has to be synodal; it should involve a "journeying together" that values "the charisms that the Spirit bestows in accordance with the vocation and role of each of the Church's members, through a process of co-responsibility . . . Motivated by this spirit, we can move toward a participatory and co-responsible Church, one capable of appreciating its own rich variety, gratefully accepting the contributions of the lay faithful, including young people and women, consecrated persons, as well as groups, associations and movements. No one should be excluded or exclude themselves."[111]

207. In this way, by learning from one another, we can better reflect that wonderful multifaceted reality that Christ's Church is meant to be. She will be able to attract young people, for her unity is not monolithic, but rather a network of varied gifts that the Spirit ceaselessly pours out upon her, renewing her and lifting her up from her poverty.

---

111 FD, no. 123.

208. In the Synod, many concrete proposals emerged for renewing youth ministry and freeing it from approaches that are no longer effective because they are incapable of entering into dialogue with contemporary youth culture. Naturally, I cannot list them all here. A number of them can be found in the Final Document of the Synod.

## MAIN COURSES OF ACTION

209. I wish simply to emphasize that youth ministry involves two main courses of action. One is *outreach*, the way we attract new young people to an experience of the Lord. The other is *growth*, the way we help those who have already had that experience to mature in it.

210. As for *outreach*, I trust that young people themselves know how best to find appealing ways to come together. They know how to organize events, sports competitions and ways to evangelize using social media, through text messages, songs, videos and other ways. They only have to be encouraged and given the freedom to be enthused about evangelizing other young people wherever they are to be found. When the message is first brought up, whether at a youth retreat, in a conversation at a bar, on school holidays, or in any of God's mysterious ways, it can awaken a deep experience of faith. What is most important, though, is that each young person can be daring enough to sow the seed of the message on that fertile terrain that is the heart of another young person.

211. In this outreach, we need to use above all the language of closeness, the language of generous, relational and existential love that touches the heart, impacts life, and awakens hope and desires. Young people need to be approached with the grammar of love, not by being preached at. The language that young people understand is spoken by those who radiate life, by those who are there for them and with them. And those who, for all their limitations

and weaknesses, try to live their faith with integrity. We also have to give greater thought to ways of incarnating the *kerygma* in the language of today's youth.

212. As for *growth*, I would make one important point. In some places, it happens that young people are helped to have a powerful experience of God, an encounter with Jesus that touched their hearts. But the only follow-up to this is a series of "formation" meetings featuring talks about doctrinal and moral issues, the evils of today's world, the Church, her social doctrine, chastity, marriage, birth control and so on. As a result, many young people get bored, they lose the fire of their encounter with Christ and the joy of following him; many give up and others become downcast or negative. Rather than being too concerned with communicating a great deal of doctrine, let us first try to awaken and consolidate the great experiences that sustain the Christian life. In the words of Romano Guardini, "when we experience a great love . . . everything else becomes part of it."[112]

213. Any educational project or path of growth for young people must certainly include formation in Christian doctrine and morality. It is likewise important that it have two main goals. One is the development of the *kerygma*, the foundational experience of encounter with God through Christ's death and resurrection. The other is growth in fraternal love, community life and service.

214. This was something I emphasized in *Evangelii Gaudium*, and I consider it worth repeating here. It would be a serious mistake to think that in youth ministry "the kerygma should give way to a supposedly more 'solid' formation. Nothing is more solid, profound, secure, meaningful and wisdom-filled than that initial proclamation. All Christian formation consists of entering more deeply into the kerygma"[113] and incarnating it ever more fully in our lives.

112 *Das Wesen des Christentums. Die neue Wirklichkeit des Herrn*, Mainz, 7th ed., 1991, 14.
113 No. 165: AAS 105 (2013), 1089.

Consequently, youth ministry should always include occasions for renewing and deepening our personal experience of the love of God and the living Christ. It can do this in a variety of ways: testimonies, songs, moments of adoration, times of spiritual reflection on the sacred Scriptures, and even an intelligent use of social networks. Yet this joyful experience of encounter with the Lord should never be replaced by a kind of "indoctrination."

215. On the other hand, any program of youth ministry should clearly incorporate various means and resources that can help young people grow in fraternity, to live as brothers and sisters, to help one another, to build community, to be of service to others, to be close to the poor. If fraternal love is the "new commandment" (Jn 13:34), "the fullness of the Law" (Rom 13:10) and our best way of showing our love for God, then it has to have a primary place in every project of youth formation and growth to maturity.

## SUITABLE ENVIRONMENTS

216. We need to make all our institutions better equipped to be more welcoming to young people, since so many have a real sense of being orphaned. Here I am not referring to family problems but to something experienced by boys and girls, young people and adults, parents and children alike. To all these orphans—including perhaps ourselves—communities like a parish or school should offer possibilities for experiencing openness and love, affirmation and growth. Many young people today feel that they have inherited the failed dreams of their parents and grandparents, dreams betrayed by injustice, social violence, selfishness and lack of concern for others. In a word, they feel uprooted. If the young grow up in a world in ashes, it will be hard for them to keep alive the flame of great dreams and projects. If they grow up in a desert devoid of meaning, where will they develop a desire to devote their lives to sowing seeds? The experience of discontinuity, uprootedness and the

collapse of fundamental certainties, fostered by today's media culture, creates a deep sense of orphanhood to which we must respond by creating an attractive and fraternal environment where others can live with a sense of purpose.

217. In a word, to create a "home" is to create "a family." "It is to learn to feel connected to others by more than merely utilitarian and practical bonds, to be united in such a way as to feel that our life is a bit more human. To create a home is to let prophecy take flesh and make our hours and days less cold, less indifferent and anonymous. It is to create bonds by simple, everyday acts that all of us can perform. A home, as we all know, demands that everyone work together. No one can be indifferent or stand apart, since each is a stone needed to build the home. This also involves asking the Lord to grant us the grace to learn how to be patient, to forgive one another, to start over each day. How many times should I forgive and start over? Seventy times seven times, as many times as necessary. To create strong bonds requires confidence and trust nurtured daily by patience and forgiveness. And that is how the miracle takes place: we feel that here we are reborn, here we are all reborn, because we feel God's caress that enables us to dream of a more human world, and therefore of a world more divine."[114]

218. Along these lines, our institutions should provide young people with places they can make their own, where they can come and go freely, feel welcome and readily meet other young people, whether at times of difficulty and frustration, or of joy and celebration. Some of this is already happening in oratories and other youth centres, which in many cases offer a friendly and relaxed setting where friendships can grow, where young men and women can meet one another, where they can share music, games, sports, but also reflection and prayer. In such places, much can be offered, without great expenditure of funds. Then too, the person-to-person contact

---

114 *Address at the Visit to the Good Samaritan Home, Panama,* (January 27, 2019): *L'Osservatore Romano,* January 28-29, 2019, 10.

indispensable for passing on the message can happen, something whose place cannot be taken by any pastoral resource or strategy.

219. "Friendship and discussion, often within more or less structured groups, offer the opportunity to strengthen social and relational skills in a context in which one is neither analyzed nor judged. Group experience is also a great resource for sharing the faith and for mutual help in bearing witness. The young are able to guide other young people and to exercise a genuine apostolate among their friends."[115]

220. This is not to say that they should become isolated and lose all contact with parish communities, movements and other ecclesial institutions. But they will be better integrated into communities that are open, living their faith, eager to radiate Christ, joyful, free, fraternal and committed. These communities can be settings where they feel that it is possible to cultivate precious relationships.

## YOUTH MINISTRY IN EDUCATIONAL INSTITUTIONS

221. Schools are unquestionably a platform for drawing close to children and young people. Precisely because they are such privileged places of personal development, the Christian community has always been concerned to train teachers and administrators, and to found its own schools of various kinds and levels. In this field of educating the young, the Spirit has raised up countless charisms and examples of holiness. Yet schools are in urgent need of self-criticism, if we consider the results of their pastoral outreach, which in many cases focuses on a kind of religious instruction that proves often incapable of nurturing lasting experiences of faith. Some Catholic schools seem to be structured only for the sake of self-preservation. Fear of change makes them entrenched and defensive before the dangers, real or imagined, that any change might bring. A school that becomes a "bunker," protecting its students

---
115 FD, no. 36.

from errors "from without" is a caricature of this tendency. Yet this image reflects, in a chilling way, what many young people experience when they graduate from certain educational institutions: an insurmountable disconnect between what they were taught and the world in which they live. The way they were instructed in religious and moral values did not prepare them to uphold those values in a world that holds them up to ridicule, nor did they learn ways of praying and practicing the faith that can be easily sustained amid the fast pace of today's society. For one of the greatest joys that any educator can have is to see a student turn into a strong, well-integrated person, a leader, someone prepared to give.

222. Catholic schools remain essential places for the evangelization of the young. Account should be taken of a number of guiding principles set forth in *Veritatis Gaudium* for the renewal and revival of missionary outreach on the part of schools and universities. These include a fresh experience of the *kerygma*, wide-ranging dialogue, interdisciplinary and cross-disciplinary approaches, the promotion of a culture of encounter, the urgency of creating networks and an option in favor of those who are least, those whom society discards.[116] Similarly important is the ability to integrate the knowledge of head, heart and hands.

223. On the other hand, we cannot separate spiritual from cultural formation. The Church has always sought to develop ways of providing the young with the best education possible. Nor should she stop now, for young people have a right to it. "Today, above all, the right to a good education means protecting wisdom, that is, knowledge that is human and humanizing. All too often we are conditioned by trivial and fleeting models of life that drive us to pursue success at a low price, discrediting sacrifice and inculcating the idea that education is not necessary unless it immediately provides concrete results. No, education makes us raise questions, keeps us from

---

116 Cf. Apostolic Constitution *Veritatis Gaudium* (December 8, 2017), no. 4: AAS 110 (2018), 7-8.

being anaesthetized by banality, and impels us to pursue meaning in life. We need to reclaim our right not to be sidetracked by the many sirens that nowadays distract from this pursuit. Ulysses, in order not to give in to the siren song that bewitched his sailors and made them crash against the rocks, tied himself to the mast of the ship and had his companions plug their ears. Orpheus, on the other hand, did something else to counter the siren song: he intoned an even more beautiful melody, which enchanted the sirens. This, then, is your great challenge: to respond to the crippling refrains of cultural consumerism with thoughtful and firm decisions, with research, knowledge and sharing."[117]

## AREAS NEEDING TO BE DEVELOPED

224. Many young people have come to appreciate silence and close-ness to God. Groups that gather to adore the Blessed Sacrament or to pray with the word of God have also increased. We should never underestimate the ability of young people to be open to contempla-tive prayer. We need only find the right ways and means to help them embark on this precious experience. When it comes to worship and prayer, "in many settings, young Catholics are asking for prayer opportunities and sacramental celebrations capable of speaking to their daily lives through a fresh, authentic and joyful liturgy."[118] It is important to make the most of the great moments of the liturgical year, particularly Holy Week, Pentecost and Christmas. But other festive occasions can provide a welcome break in their routine and help them experience the joy of faith.

225. Christian service represents a unique opportunity for growth and openness to God's gifts of faith and charity. Many young peo-ple are attracted by the possibility of helping others, especially chil-dren and the poor. Often this service is the first step to a discovery

---

117 *Address at the Meeting with Students and Representatives of the Academic World in Piazza San Domenico, Bologna* (October 1, 2017): AAS 109 (2017), 1115.

118 FD, no. 51.

or rediscovery of life in Christ and the Church. Many young people grow weary of our programs of doctrinal and spiritual formation, and at times demand a chance to be active participants in activities that benefit others.

226. Nor can we overlook the importance of the arts, like theatre, painting, and others. "Music is particularly important, representing as it does a real environment in which the young are constantly immersed, as well as a culture and a language capable of arousing emotion and shaping identity. The language of music also represents a pastoral resource with a particular bearing on the liturgy and its renewal."[119] Singing can be a great incentive to young people as they make their way through life. As St. Augustine says: "Sing, but continue on your journey. Do not grow lazy, but sing to make the way more enjoyable. Sing, but keep going . . . If you make progress, you will continue your journey, but be sure that your progress is in virtue, true faith and right living. Sing then, and keep walking."[120]

227. "Equally significant is the emphasis that young people place on sports; the Church should not underestimate the potential of sports for education and formation, but instead maintain a strong presence there. The world of sport needs to be helped to overcome some of its problematic aspects, such as the idolization of champions, subservience to commercial interests and the ideology of success at any cost."[121] At the heart of the experience of sport is "joy: the joy of exercising, of being together, of being alive and rejoicing in the gifts the Creator gives us each day."[122] Some Fathers of the Church used the example of the training of athletes to encourage the young to develop their strength and to overcome idleness and boredom. St. Basil the Great, writing to young people, used the

119 Ibid., 47.

120 Sermo 256, 3: PL 38, 1193.

121 FD, no. 47.

122 Address to a Delegation of the International Special Olympics (February 16, 2017): L'Osservatore Romano, February 17, 2017, 8.

effort demanded by athletics to illustrate the value of self-sacrifice as a means of growth in virtue: "These men endure sufferings beyond number, they use many means to build their strength, they sweat constantly as they train . . . in a word, they so discipline themselves that their whole life prior to the contest is but a preparation for it . . . How then can we, who have been promised rewards so wondrous in number and in splendor that no tongue can recount them, even think of winning them if we do nothing other than spend our lives in leisure and make but half-hearted efforts?"[123]

228. Nature holds a special attraction for many adolescents and young people who recognize our need to care for the environment. Such is the case with the scouting movement and other groups that encourage closeness to nature, camping trips, hiking, expeditions and campaigns to improve the environment. In the spirit of St. Francis of Assisi, these experiences can be a real initiation into the school of universal fraternity and contemplative prayer.

229. These and various other opportunities for evangelizing the young should not make us forget that, despite the changing times and sensibilities of young people, there are gifts of God that never grow old, for they contain a power transcending all times and places. There is the word of the Lord, ever living and effective, the nourishing presence of Christ in the Eucharist, and the sacrament of Reconciliation, which brings us freedom and strength. We can also mention the inexhaustible spiritual riches preserved by the Church in the witness of her saints and the teaching of the great spiritual masters. Although we have to respect different stages of growth, and at times need to wait patiently for the right moment, we cannot fail to invite young people to drink from these wellsprings of new life. We have no right to deprive them of this great good.

---

123 *Ad Adolescentes*, VIII, 11-12: PG 31, 580.

# A "POPULAR" YOUTH MINISTRY

230. In addition to the ordinary, well-planned pastoral ministry that parishes and movements carry out, it is also important to allow room for a "popular" youth ministry, with a different style, schedule, pace and method. Broader and more flexible, it goes out to those places where real young people are active, and fosters the natural leadership qualities and the charisms sown by the Holy Spirit. It tries to avoid imposing obstacles, rules, controls and obligatory structures on these young believers who are natural leaders in their neighborhoods and in other settings. We need only to accompany and encourage them, trusting a little more in the genius of the Holy Spirit, who acts as he wills.

231. We are speaking of truly "popular" leaders, not elitists or those closed off in small groups of select individuals. To be able to generate a "popular" ministry to youth, "they need to learn to listen to the sense of the people, to become their spokespersons and to work for their promotion."[124] When we speak of "the people," we are not speaking about the structures of society or the Church, but about all those persons who journey, not as individuals, but as a closely-bound community of all and for all, one that refuses to leave the poor and the vulnerable behind. "The people wants everyone to share in the common good and thus agree to keep pace with its least members, so that all can arrive together."[125] "Popular" leaders, then, are those able to make everyone, including the poor, the vulnerable, the frail and the wounded, part of the forward march of youth. They do not shun or fear those young people who have experienced hurt or borne the weight of the cross.

---

124 Episcopal Conference of Argentina, *Declaración de San Miguel*, Buenos Aires, 1969, X, 1.

125 Rafael Tello, *La nueva evangelización*, II (Appendices I and II), Buenos Aires, 2013, 111.

232. Similarly, especially in the case of young people who do not come from Christian families or institutions, and are slowly growing to maturity, we have to encourage all the good that we can.[126] Christ warned us not to see only the good grain (cf. Mt 13:24-30). At times, in the attempt to develop a pure and perfect youth ministry, marked by abstract ideas, protected from the world and free of every flaw, we can turn the Gospel into a dull, meaningless and unattractive proposition. Such a youth ministry ends up completely removed from the world of young people and suited only to an elite Christian youth that sees itself as different, while living in an empty and unproductive isolation. In rejecting the weeds, we also uproot or choke any number of shoots trying to spring up in spite of their limitations.

233. Instead of "overwhelming young people with a body of rules that make Christianity seem reductive and moralistic, we are called to invest in their fearlessness and to train them to take up their responsibilities, in the sure knowledge that error, failure and crisis are experiences that can strengthen their humanity."[127]

234. The Synod called for the development of a youth ministry capable of being inclusive, with room for all kinds of young people, to show that we are a Church with open doors. Nor does one have to accept fully all the teachings of the Church to take part in certain of our activities for young people. It is enough to have an open mind toward all those who have the desire and willingness to be encountered by God's revealed truth. Some of our pastoral activities can assume that a journey of faith has already begun, but we need a "popular" youth ministry that can open doors and make room for everyone, with their doubts and frustrations, their problems and their efforts to find themselves, their past errors, their experiences of sin and all their difficulties.

---

126 Cf. Apostolic Exhortation *Evangelii Gaudium* (November 24, 2013), nos. 44-45: AAS 105 (2013), 1038-1039.

127 FD, no. 70.

235. Room should also be made for "all those who have other visions of life, who belong to other religions or who distance themselves from religion altogether. All the young, without exception, are in God's heart and thus in the Church's heart. We recognize frankly that this statement on our lips does not always find real expression in our pastoral actions: often we remain closed in our environments, where their voice does not penetrate, or else we dedicate ourselves to less demanding and more enjoyable activities, suppressing that healthy pastoral restlessness that would urge us to move out from our supposed security. The Gospel also asks us to be daring, and we want to be so, without presumption and without proselytizing, testifying to the love of the Lord and stretching out our hands to all the young people in the world."[128]

236. Youth ministry, when it ceases to be elitist and is willing to be "popular," is a process that is gradual, respectful, patient, hopeful, tireless and compassionate. The Synod proposed the example of the disciples of Emmaus (cf. Lk 24:13-35) as a model of what happens in youth ministry.

237. "Jesus walks with two disciples who did not grasp the meaning of all that happened to him, and are leaving Jerusalem and the community behind. Wanting to accompany them, he joins them on the way. He asks them questions and listens patiently to their version of events, and in this way he helps them *recognize* what they were experiencing. Then, with affection and power, he proclaims the word to them, leading them to *interpret* the events they had experienced in the light of the Scriptures. He accepts their invitation to stay with them as evening falls; he enters into their night. As they listen to him speak, their hearts burn within them and their minds are opened; they then recognize him in the breaking of the bread. They themselves *choose* to resume their journey at once

---

128  Ibid., no. 117.

84

in the opposite direction, to return to the community and to share the experience of their encounter with the risen Lord."[129]

238. Various manifestations of popular piety, especially pilgrimages, attract young people who do not readily feel at home in ecclesial structures, and represent a concrete sign of their trust in God. These ways of seeking God are seen particularly in young people who are poor, but also those in other sectors of society. They should not be looked down on, but encouraged and promoted. Popular piety "is a legitimate way of living the faith"[130] and "an expression of the spontaneous missionary activity of the People of God."[131]

## ALWAYS MISSIONARIES

239. Here I would point out that it doesn't take much to make young people missionaries. Even those who are most frail, limited and troubled can be missionaries in their own way, for goodness can always be shared, even if it exists alongside many limitations. A young person who makes a pilgrimage to ask Our Lady for help, and invites a friend or companion along, by that single gesture is being a good missionary. Inseparable from a "popular" youth ministry is an irrepressible "popular" missionary activity that breaks through our customary models and ways of thinking. Let us accompany and encourage it, but not presume to overly regulate it.

240. If we can hear what the Spirit is saying to us, we have to realize that youth ministry is always missionary. Young people are greatly enriched when they overcome their reticence and dare to visit homes, and in this way make contact with people's lives. They learn how to look beyond their family and their group of friends, and they gain a broader vision of life. At the same time, their faith

---

129  Ibid., no. 4.

130  Apostolic Exhortation *Evangelii Gaudium* (November 24, 2013), no. 124: AAS 105 (2013), 1072.

131  Ibid., no. 122, 1071.

and their sense of being part of the Church grow stronger. Youth missions, which usually take place during school holidays after a period of preparation, can lead to a renewed experience of faith and even serious thoughts about a vocation.

241. Young people can find new fields for mission in the most varied settings. For example, since they are already so familiar with social networks, they should be encouraged to fill them with God, fraternity and commitment.

## ACCOMPANIMENT BY ADULTS

242. Young people need to have their freedom respected, yet they also need to be accompanied. The family should be the first place of accompaniment. Youth ministry can present the ideal of life in Christ as the process of building a house on rock (cf. Mt 7:24-25). For most young people, that house, their life, will be built on marriage and married love. That is why youth ministry and the pastoral care of families should be coordinated and integrated, with the aim of ensuring a continuous and suitable accompaniment of the vocational process.

243. The community has an important role in the accompaniment of young people; it should feel collectively responsible for accepting, motivating, encouraging and challenging them. All should regard young people with understanding, appreciation and affection, and avoid constantly judging them or demanding of them a perfection beyond their years.

244. At the Synod, "many pointed to the shortage of qualified people devoted to accompaniment. Belief in the theological and pastoral value of listening entails rethinking and renewing the ways that priestly ministry is ordinarily exercised, and reviewing its priorities. The Synod also recognized the need to train consecrated persons and laypeople, male and female, to accompany young people. The

charism of listening that the Holy Spirit calls forth within the communities might also receive institutional recognition as a form of ecclesial service."[132]

245. There is also a special need to accompany young men and women showing leadership potential, so that they can receive training and the necessary qualifications. The young people who met before the Synod called for "programs for the formation and continued development of young leaders. Some young women feel that there is a lack of leading female role models within the Church and they too wish to give their intellectual and professional gifts to the Church. We also believe that seminarians and religious should have an even greater ability to accompany young leaders."[133]

246. The same young people described to us the qualities they hope to find in a mentor, and they expressed this with much clarity. "The qualities of such a mentor include: being a faithful Christian who engages with the Church and the world; someone who constantly seeks holiness; someone who is a confidant without judging. Similarly, someone who actively listens to the needs of young people and responds in kind; someone deeply loving and self-aware; someone who recognizes his or her limits and knows the joys and sorrows of the spiritual journey. An especially important quality in mentors is the acknowledgement of their own humanity—the fact that they are human beings who make mistakes: not perfect people but forgiven sinners. Sometimes mentors are put on a pedestal, and when they fall, it may have a devastating impact on young people's ability to continue to engage with the Church. Mentors should not lead young people as passive followers, but walk alongside them, allowing them to be active participants in the journey. They should respect the freedom that comes with a young person's process of discernment and equip them with tools to do so well. A mentor should

---

132 FD, no. 9.

133 *Document of the Pre-Synodal Meeting for the Preparation of the XV Ordinary Assembly of the Synod of Bishops*, Rome (March 24, 2018), 12.

believe wholeheartedly in a young person's ability to participate in the life of the Church. A mentor should therefore nurture the seeds of faith in young people, without expecting to immediately see the fruits of the work of the Holy Spirit. This role is not and cannot be limited to priests and consecrated life, but the laity should also be empowered to take on such a role. All such mentors should benefit from being well-formed, and engage in ongoing formation."[134]

247. The Church's educational institutions are undoubtedly a communal setting for accompaniment; they can offer guidance to many young people, especially when they "seek to welcome all young people, regardless of their religious choices, cultural origins and personal, family or social situations. In this way, the Church makes a fundamental contribution to the integral education of the young in various parts of the world."[135] They would curtail this role unduly were they to lay down rigid criteria for students to enter and remain in them, since they would deprive many young people of an accompaniment that could help enrich their lives.

134  Ibid., 10.
135  FD, no. 15.

# CHAPTER EIGHT

# Vocation

248. The word "vocation" can be understood in a broad sense as a calling from God, including the call to life, the call to friendship with him, the call to holiness, and so forth. This is helpful, since it situates our whole life in relation to the God who loves us. It makes us realize that nothing is the result of pure chance but that everything in our lives can become a way of responding to the Lord, who has a wonderful plan for us.

249. In the Exhortation *Gaudete et Exsultate*, I spoke about the vocation of all to grow and mature for the glory of God; I wanted "to repropose the call to holiness in a practical way for our own time, with all its risks, challenges and opportunities."[136] The Second Vatican Council helped us to recognize anew this call addressed to each of us: "All the faithful, whatever their condition or state, are called by the Lord, each in his or her own way, to that perfect holiness by which the Father himself is perfect."[137]

## GOD'S CALL TO FRIENDSHIP

250. The first thing we need to discern and discover is this: Jesus wants to be a friend to every young person. This discernment is the basis of all else. In the risen Lord's dialogue with Simon Peter, his great question was: "Simon, son of John, do you love me?" (Jn 21:16). In other words, do you love me as a friend? The mission that Peter received to shepherd Jesus' flock will always be linked to this gratuitous love, this love of friendship.

---

136 Apostolic Exhortation *Gaudete et Exsultate* (March 19, 2018), no. 2.

137 Dogmatic Constitution on the Church *Lumen Gentium*, no. 11.

251. On the other hand, there was the unsuccessful encounter of Jesus and the rich young man, which clearly shows that the young man failed to perceive the Lord's loving gaze (cf. Mk 10:21). He went away sorrowful, despite his original good intentions, because he could not turn his back on his many possessions (cf. Mt 19:22). He missed the opportunity of what surely would have been a great friendship. We will never know what that one young man, upon whom Jesus gazed with love and to whom he stretched out his hand, might have been for us, what he might have done for mankind.

252. "The life that Jesus gives us is a love story, a *life history* that wants to blend with ours and sink roots in the soil of our own lives. That life is not salvation up 'in the cloud' and waiting to be downloaded, a new 'app' to be discovered, or a technique of mental self-improvement. Still less is that life a 'tutorial' for finding out the latest news. The salvation that God offers us is *an invitation to be part of a love story* interwoven with our personal stories; it is alive and wants to be born in our midst so that we can bear fruit just as we are, wherever we are and with everyone all around us. The Lord comes there to sow and to be sown."[138]

## BEING THERE FOR OTHERS

253. I would now like to speak of vocation in the strict sense, as a call to missionary service to others. The Lord calls us to share in his work of creation and to contribute to the common good by using the gifts we have received.

254. This missionary vocation thus has to do with service. For our life on earth reaches full stature when it becomes an offering. Here I would repeat that "the mission of being in the heart of the people is not just a part of my life or a badge I can take off; it is not an 'extra' or just another moment in life. Instead, it is something I cannot

---

138 *Address at the Vigil, XXXIV World Youth Day in Panama* (January 26, 2019): *L'Osservatore Romano*, January 28-29, 2019, 6.

uproot from my being without destroying my very self. I am a mission on this earth; that is the reason why I am here in this world."[139] It follows that every form of pastoral activity, formation and spirituality should be seen in the light of our Christian vocation.

255. Your own personal vocation does not consist only in the work you do, though that is an expression of it. Your vocation is something more: it is a path guiding your many efforts and actions toward service to others. So in discerning your vocation, it is important to determine if you see in yourself the abilities needed to perform that specific service to society.

256. This gives greater value to everything you do. Your work stops being just about making money, keeping busy or pleasing others. It becomes your vocation because you are called to it; it is something more than merely a pragmatic decision. In the end, it is a recognition of why I was made, why I am here on earth, and what the Lord's plan is for my life. He will not show me every place, time and detail, since I will have to make my own prudent decisions about these. But he will show me a direction in life, for he is my Creator and I need to listen to his voice, so that, like clay in the hands of a potter, I can let myself be shaped and guided by him. Then I will become what I was meant to be, faithful to my own reality.

257. To respond to our vocation, we need to foster and develop all that we are. This has nothing to do with inventing ourselves or creating ourselves out of nothing. It has to do with finding our true selves in the light of God and letting our lives flourish and bear fruit. "In God's plan, every man and woman is meant to seek self-fulfillment, for every human life is called to some task by God."[140] Your vocation inspires you to bring out the best in yourself for the

---

139 Apostolic Exhortation *Evangelii Gaudium* (November 24, 2013), no. 273: AAS 105 (2013), 1130.

140 St. Paul VI, Encyclical Letter *Populorum Progressio* (March 26, 1967), no. 15: AAS 59 (1967), 265.

glory of God and the good of others. It is not simply a matter of doing things, but of doing them with meaning and direction. St. Alberto Hurtado told young people to think very seriously about the direction their lives should take: "If the helmsman of a ship becomes careless, he is fired straightaway for not taking his sacred responsibility seriously. As for our lives, are we fully aware of the course they are taking? What course is your life taking? If it is necessary to give this more thought, I would beg each one of you to give it the highest consideration, because to get it right is tantamount to success; to err is quite simply to fail."[141]

258. In the life of each young person, this "being there for others" normally has to do with two basic issues: forming a new family and working. Surveys of young people repeatedly confirm that these are the two major issues worrying them and, at the same time, exciting them. Both must be the object of particular discernment. Let us look briefly at each of them.

## LOVE AND FAMILY

259. Young people intensely feel the call to love; they dream of meeting the right person with whom they can form a family and build a life together. This is undoubtedly a vocation which God himself makes known to them through their feelings, desires and dreams. I dwelt more fully on this theme in the Apostolic Exhortation *Amoris Laetitia*. I would encourage all young people to read especially the fourth and fifth chapters of that Exhortation.

260. I like to think that "two Christians who marry have recognized the call of the Lord in their own love story, the vocation to form one flesh and one life from two, male and female. The Sacrament of Holy Matrimony envelops this love in the grace of God; it roots it in God himself. By this gift, and by the certainty of this call, you

---

141 *Meditación de Semana Santa para jóvenes*, written aboard a cargo ship returning from the United States in 1946: *https://www.padrealbertohurtado.cl/escritos-2/*.

can go forward with assurance; you have nothing to fear; you can face everything together!"[142]

261. Here, we need to remember that God created us as sexual beings. He himself "created sexuality, which is a marvelous gift to his creatures."[143] Within the vocation to marriage we should acknowledge and appreciate that "sexuality, sex, is a gift from God. It is not taboo. It is a gift from God, a gift the Lord gives us. It has two purposes: to love and to generate life. It is passion, passionate love. True love is passionate. Love between a man and a woman, when it is passionate, always leads to giving life. Always. To give life with body and soul."[144]

262. The Synod insisted that "the family continues to be the principal point of reference for young people. Children appreciate the love and care of their parents, they give importance to family bonds, and they hope to succeed in forming a family when it is their time. Without doubt, the increase of separation, divorce, second unions and single-parent families can cause great suffering and a crisis of identity in young people. Sometimes they must take on responsibilities that are not proportioned to their age and that force them to become adults before their time. Often, grandparents are a crucial aid in affection and religious education: with their wisdom they are a vital link in the relationship between generations."[145]

263. It is true that the difficulties they experience in their own family can lead many young people to ask whether it is worthwhile to start a new family, to be faithful, to be generous. I can tell you that it certainly is. It is worth your every effort to invest in the family;

---

142 *Meeting with the Young People of Umbria in Assisi* (October 4, 2013): AAS 105 (2013), 921.

143 Post-Synodal Apostolic Exhortation *Amoris Laetitia* (March 19, 2016), 150: AAS 108 (2016), 369.

144 *Address to Young People from the Diocese of Grenoble-Vienne* (September 17, 2018): *L'Osservatore Romano*, September 19, 2018, 8.

145 FD, no. 32.

there you will find the best incentives to mature and the greatest joys to experience and share. Don't let yourselves be robbed of a great love. Don't let yourselves be led astray by those who propose a life of rampant individualism that in the end leads to isolation and the worst sort of loneliness.

264. Today, a culture of the ephemeral dominates, but it is an illusion. To think that nothing can be definitive is a deceptive lie. "Today, there are those who say that marriage is out of fashion . . . In a culture of relativism and the ephemeral, many preach the importance of 'enjoying' the present moment. They say that it is not worth making a lifelong commitment, making a definitive decision . . . I ask you, instead, to be revolutionaries, I ask you to swim against the tide; yes, I am asking you to rebel against this culture that sees everything as temporary and that ultimately believes you are incapable of responsibility, incapable of true love."[146] I have great confidence in you, and for this very reason, I urge you to opt for marriage.

265. Marriage requires preparation, and this calls for growing in self-knowledge, developing the greater virtues, particularly love, patience, openness to dialogue and helping others. It also involves maturing in your own sexuality, so that it can become less and less a means of using others, and increasingly a capacity to entrust yourself fully to another person in an exclusive and generous way.

266. As the bishops of Colombia have taught, "Christ knows that spouses are not perfect and that they need to overcome their weakness and lack of constancy so that their love can grow and endure. For this reason, he grants spouses his grace, which is at once light

---

146 *Meeting with Volunteers, XXVIII World Youth Day in Rio de Janeiro* (July 28, 2013): *Insegnamenti* 1, 2 (2013), 125.

and the strength enabling them to achieve progressively their ideal of married life in accordance with God's plan."[147]

267. For those who are not called to marriage or the consecrated life, it must always be remembered that the first and most important vocation is the vocation we have received in baptism. Those who are single, even if not by their own choice, can offer a particular witness to that vocation through their own path of personal growth.

# WORK

268. The bishops of the United States have pointed out that "young adulthood often signals a person's entrance into the world of work. 'What do you do for a living?' is a constant topic of conversation because work is a major part of their lives. For young adults, this experience is highly fluid because they move from job to job and even from career to career. Work can dictate their use of time and can determine what they can afford to do or buy. It can also determine the quality and quantity of leisure time. Work defines and influences a young adult's identity and self-concept and is a prime place where friendships and other relationships develop because generally it is not done alone. Young men and women speak of work as fulfilling a function and providing meaning. Work allows young adults to meet their practical needs but even more importantly to seek meaning and fulfillment of their dreams and visions. Although work may not help achieve their dreams, it is important for young adults to nurture a vision, learn how to work in a truly personal and life-giving way, and to continue to discern God's call."[148]

269. I ask young people not to expect to live without working, depending on others for help. This is not good, because "work is a

---

147 Episcopal Conference of Colombia, *Mensaje Cristiano sobre el matrimonio* (May 14, 1981).

148 United States Conference of Catholic Bishops, *Sons and Daughters of Light: A Pastoral Plan for Ministry with Young Adults*, November 12, 1996, Part One, 3.

necessity, part of the meaning of life on this earth, a path to growth, human development and personal fulfillment. In this sense, helping the poor financially must always be a provisional solution in the face of pressing needs."[149] Hence, "together with the awe-filled contemplation of creation which we find in St. Francis of Assisi, the Christian spiritual tradition has also developed a rich and balanced understanding of the meaning of work, as, for example, in the life of Bl. Charles de Foucauld and his followers."[150]

270. The Synod noted that in the area of work, young people can "experience forms of exclusion and marginalization, of which the first and most serious is youth unemployment, which in some countries reaches exorbitant levels. Besides making them poor, the lack of work impacts negatively on young people's capacity to dream and to hope, and it deprives them of the possibility of contributing to the development of society. In many countries, this situation depends on the fact that some sectors of the young population lack adequate professional skills, perhaps because of deficiencies in the system of education and training. Often job insecurity among the young is linked to economic interests that exploit labor."[151]

271. This is a highly complex and sensitive issue that politics must make a priority, especially at present, when the speed of technological advances and the concern to reduce labor costs can lead quickly to the replacement of many jobs by machines. It is also a crucial societal issue because employment for a young person is not merely a means of making money. Work is an expression of human dignity, a path of development and of social inclusion. It is a constant stimulus to grow in responsibility and creativity, a protection against the tendency toward individualism and personal gratification. At

---

149 Encyclical Letter *Laudato Si'* (May 24, 2015), no. 128: AAS 107 (2015), 898.

150 Ibid., no. 125: AAS 107 (2015), 897.

151 FD, no. 40.

the same time, it is an opportunity to give glory to God by developing one's abilities.

272. Young people do not always have the chance to decide what kind of work they will do, or how their energies and talents will be spent. Because, alongside their own aspirations, abilities and choices, there is the harsh reality of the job market. It is true that you cannot live without working, and that sometimes you have to accept whatever is available, but I ask you never to give up on your dreams, never completely bury a calling, and never accept defeat. Keep seeking at least partial or imperfect ways to live what you have discerned to be your real calling.

273. When we discover that God is calling us to something, that this or that is what we were made for—whether it be nursing, carpentry, communication, engineering, teaching, art or any other kind of work—then we will be able to summon up our best capacities for sacrifice, generosity and dedication. Knowing that we don't do things just for the sake of doing them, but rather we endow them with meaning, as a response to a call that resounds in the depth of our being to offer something to others: that is what makes these occupations bring a sense of deep fulfillment. As we read in the ancient biblical book of Ecclesiastes: "I saw that there is nothing better than that a man should enjoy his work" (3:22).

# THE VOCATION TO SPECIAL CONSECRATION

274. If we are indeed convinced that the Holy Spirit continues to inspire vocations to the priesthood and the religious life, we can "once more cast out the nets" in the Lord's name, with complete confidence. We can dare, as we should, to tell each young person to ask whether this is the path that they are meant to follow.

275. Occasionally, I would bring this up with young people, and they would respond almost jokingly: "No, that's not for me!" Yet,

a few years later, some of them were in the seminary. The Lord cannot fail in his promise to provide the Church with shepherds, for without them she would not be able to live and carry out her mission. If it is true that some priests do not give good witness, that does not mean that the Lord stops calling. On the contrary, he doubles the stakes, for he never ceases to care for his beloved Church.

276. In discerning your vocation, do not dismiss the possibility of devoting yourself to God in the priesthood, the religious life or in other forms of consecration. Why not? You can be sure that, if you do recognize and follow a call from God, there you will find complete fulfillment.

277. Jesus is walking in our midst, as he did in Galilee. He walks through our streets, and he quietly stops and looks into our eyes. His call is attractive and intriguing. Yet today the stress and quick pace of a world constantly bombarding us with stimuli can leave no room for that interior silence in which we can perceive Jesus' gaze and hear his call. In the meantime, many attractively packaged offers will come your way. They may seem appealing and exciting, although in time they will only leave you feeling empty, weary and alone. Don't let this happen to you, because the maelstrom of this world can drive you to take a route without real meaning, without direction, without clear goals, and thus thwart many of your efforts. It is better to seek out that calm and quiet that enable you to reflect, pray, look more clearly at the world around you, and then, with Jesus, come to recognize the vocation that is yours in this world.

# CHAPTER NINE

# Discernment

278. In the Apostolic Exhortation *Gaudete et Exsultate*, I spoke in rather general terms about discernment. I would now like to take up some of those reflections and apply them to the way we discern our own vocation in the world.

279. I mentioned there that all of us, but "especially the young, are immersed in a culture of zapping. We can navigate simultaneously on two or more screens and interact at the same time with two or three virtual scenarios. Without the wisdom of discernment, we can easily become prey to every passing trend."[152] Indeed, "this is all the more important when some novelty presents itself in our lives. Then we have to decide whether it is new wine brought by God or an illusion created by the spirit of this world or the spirit of the devil."[153]

280. Such discernment, "even though it includes reason and prudence, goes beyond them, for it seeks a glimpse of that unique and mysterious plan that God has for each of us . . . It has to do with the meaning of my life before the Father who knows and loves me, and with the real purpose of my life, which nobody knows better than he."[154]

281. Here we see the importance of the formation of conscience, which allows discernment to grow in depth and in fidelity to God: "Forming our conscience is the work of a lifetime, in which we learn to cultivate the very sentiments of Jesus Christ, adopting the

---

152  Apostolic Exhortation *Gaudete et Exsultate* (March 19, 2018), no. 167.

153  Ibid., no. 168.

154  Ibid., no. 170.

criteria behind his choices and the intentions behind his actions (cf. Phil 2:5)."[155]

282. In this process of formation, we let ourselves be transformed by Christ, even as we develop "the habit of doing good, which also is a part of our examination of conscience. We do not simply identify sins, but also recognize God's work in our daily lives, in the events of our personal history and the world around us, and in the witness of all those men and women who have gone before us or accompany us with their wisdom. This helps us to grow in the virtue of prudence and to give an overall direction to our life through concrete choices, in the serene awareness of both our gifts and our limitations."[156]

# DISCERNING YOUR VOCATION

283. A particular form of discernment involves the effort to discover our own vocation. Since this is a very personal decision that others cannot make for us, it requires a certain degree of solitude and silence. "The Lord speaks to us in a variety of ways, at work, through others and at every moment. Yet we simply cannot do without the silence of prolonged prayer, which enables us better to perceive God's language, to interpret the real meaning of the inspirations we believe we have received, to calm our anxieties and to see the whole of our existence afresh in his own light."[157]

284. Yet this silence does not make us close in on ourselves. "We must remember that prayerful discernment has to be born of an openness to listening—to the Lord and to others, and to reality itself, which always challenges us in new ways. Only if we are prepared to listen, do we have the freedom to set aside our own partial or insufficient ideas . . . In this way, we become truly open to

---

155 FD, no. 108.

156 Ibid.

157 Apostolic Exhortation *Gaudete et Exsultate* (March 19, 2018), no. 171.

accepting a call that can shatter our security, but lead us to a better life. It is not enough that everything be calm and peaceful. God may be offering us something more, but in our comfortable inadvertence, we do not recognize it."[158]

285. When seeking to discern our own vocation, there are certain questions we ought to ask. We should not start with wondering where we could make more money, or achieve greater recognition and social status. Nor even by asking what kind of work would be most pleasing to us. If we are not to go astray, we need a different starting point. We need to ask: Do I know myself, quite apart from my illusions and emotions? Do I know what brings joy or sorrow to my heart? What are my strengths and weaknesses? These questions immediately give rise to others: How can I serve people better and prove most helpful to our world and to the Church? What is my real place in this world? What can I offer to society? Even more realistic questions then follow: Do I have the abilities needed to offer this kind of service? Could I develop those abilities?

286. These questions should be centered less on ourselves and our own inclinations, but on others, so that our discernment leads us to see our life in relation to their lives. That is why I would remind you of the most important question of all. "So often in life, we waste time asking ourselves: 'Who am I?' You can keep asking, 'Who am I?' for the rest of your lives. But the real question is: 'For whom am I?'"[159] Of course, you are for God. But he has decided that you should also be for others, and he has given you many qualities, inclinations, gifts and charisms that are not for you, but to share with those around you.

---

158 Ibid., no. 172.

159 *Address of Pope Francis at the Prayer Vigil in Preparation for the XXXIV World Youth Day*, Papal Basilica of St. Mary Major (April 8, 2017): AAS 109 (2017), 447.

# THE CALL OF JESUS OUR FRIEND

287. To discern our personal vocation, we have to realize that it is a calling from a friend, who is Jesus. When we give something to our friends, we give them the best we have. It will not necessarily be what is most expensive or hard to obtain, but what we know will make them happy. Friends are so sensitive to this that they can already imagine the smile on their friend's face when he or she opens that gift. This sort of discernment that takes place among friends is what I suggest you take as a model for trying to discover God's will for your lives.

288. I want you to know that, when the Lord thinks of each of you and what he wants to give you, he sees you as his close friend. And if he plans to grant you a grace, a charism that will help you live to the full and become someone who benefits others, someone who leaves a mark in life, it will surely be a gift that will bring you more joy and excitement than anything else in this world. Not because that gift will be rare or extraordinary, but because it will perfectly fit you. It will be a perfect fit for your entire life.

289. A vocation, while a gift, will undoubtedly also be demanding. God's gifts are interactive; to enjoy them we have to be ready to take risks. Yet the demands they make are not an obligation imposed from without, but an incentive to let that gift grow and develop, and then become a gift for others. When the Lord awakens a vocation, he thinks not only of what you already are, but of what you will one day be, in his company and in that of others.

290. Sheer vitality and strength of personality combine in the hearts of young people to make them constantly aim higher. This exuberance will be tempered by time and painful experiences, but it is important for "this youthful and still untested yearning for the

infinite"[160] to encounter the unconditional friendship that Jesus offers us. More than rules and obligations, the choice that Jesus sets before us is to follow him as friends follow one another, seeking each other's company and spending time together out of pure friendship. Everything else will come in time, and even failures in life can be an invaluable way of experiencing that friendship, which will never be lost.

## LISTENING AND ACCOMPANIMENT

291. There are many priests, men and women religious, lay and professional persons, and indeed qualified young people, who can help the young with their vocational discernment. When we are called upon to help others discern their path in life, what is uppermost is the ability to listen. Listening calls for three distinct and complementary kinds of sensitivity.

292. The *first kind of sensitivity* is directed to *the individual*. It is a matter of listening to someone who is sharing his very self in what he says. A sign of this willingness to listen is the time we are ready to spare for others. More than the amount of time we spend, it is about making others feel that my time is their time, that they have all the time they need to say everything they want. The other person must sense that I am listening unconditionally, without being offended or shocked, tired or bored. We see an example of this kind of listening in the Lord; he walks alongside the disciples on the way to Emmaus, even though they are going in the wrong direction (cf. Lk 24:13-35). When Jesus says he plans to go farther, they realize that he has given them the gift of his time, so they decide to give him theirs by offering their hospitality. Attentive and selfless listening is a sign of our respect for others, whatever their ideas or their choices in life.

---

160 Romano Guardini, *Die Lebensalter. Ihre ethische und pädagogische Bedeutung*, Würzburg, 3rd ed., 1955, 20.

293. The *second kind of sensitivity* is marked by *discernment*. It tries to grasp exactly where grace or temptation is present, for sometimes the things that flit across our minds are mere temptations that can distract us from our true path. I need to ask myself what is it that the other person is trying to tell me, what they want me to realize is happening in their lives. Asking such questions helps me appreciate their thinking and the effects it has on their emotions. This kind of listening seeks to discern the salutary promptings of the good Spirit who proposes to us the Lord's truth, but also the traps laid by the evil spirit—his empty works and promises. It takes courage, warmth and tact to help others distinguish the truth from illusions or excuses.

294. The *third kind of sensitivity* is the ability to *perceive what is driving* the other person. This calls for a deeper kind of listening, one able to discern the direction in which that person truly wants to move. Apart from what they are feeling or thinking right now, and whatever has happened up to this point in their lives, the real issue is what they would like to be. This may demand that they look not to their own superficial wishes and desires, but rather to what is most pleasing to the Lord, to his plans for their life. And that is seen in a deeper inclination of the heart, beyond the surface level of their likes and feelings. This kind of listening seeks to discern their ultimate intention, the intention that definitively decides the meaning of their life. Jesus knows and appreciates this ultimate intention of the heart. He is always there, ready to help each of us to recognize it. We need but say to him: "Lord, save me! Have mercy on me!"

295. In this way, discernment becomes a genuine means of spiritual combat, helping us to follow the Lord more faithfully.[161] The desire to know our personal vocation thus takes on a supreme intensity, a different quality and higher level, one that better respects the dignity of our person and our life. In the end, good discernment is a

---

161 Cf. Apostolic Exhortation *Gaudete et Exsultate* (March 19, 2018), no. 169.

path of freedom that brings to full fruit what is unique in each person, something so personal that only God knows it. Others cannot fully understand or predict from the outside how it will develop.

296. When we listen to others in this way, at a certain moment we ourselves have to disappear in order to let the other person follow the path he or she has discovered. We have to vanish as the Lord did from the sight of his disciples in Emmaus, leaving them alone with burning hearts and an irresistible desire to set out immediately (cf. Lk 24:31-33). When they returned to the community, those disciples heard the good news that the Lord was indeed risen (cf. Lk 24:34).

297. Because "time is greater than space,"[162] we need to encourage and accompany processes, without imposing our own roadmaps. For those processes have to do with persons who remain always unique and free. There are no easy recipes, even when all the signs seem positive, since "positive factors themselves need to be subjected to a careful work of discernment, so that they do not become isolated and contradict one another, becoming absolutes and at odds with one another. The same is true for the negative factors, which are not to be rejected en bloc and without distinction, because in each one there may lie hidden some value which awaits liberation and restoration to its full truth."[163]

298. If you are to accompany others on this path, you must be the first to follow it, day in and day out. That is what Mary did, in her own youth, as she confronted her own questions and difficulties. May she renew your youthfulness by the power of her prayers and accompany you always by her maternal presence.

162 Apostolic Exhortation *Evangelii Gaudium* (November 24, 2013), no. 222: AAS 105 (2013), 1111.

163 St. John Paul II, Post-Synodal Apostolic Exhortation *Pastores Dabo Vobis* (March 25, 1992), no. 10: AAS 84 (1992), 672.

\* \* \*

# AND TO CONCLUDE . . . A WISH

299. Dear young people, my joyful hope is to see you keep running the race before you, outstripping all those who are slow or fearful. Keep running, "attracted by the face of Christ, whom we love so much, whom we adore in the Holy Eucharist and acknowledge in the flesh of our suffering brothers and sisters. May the Holy Spirit urge you on as you run this race. The Church needs your momentum, your intuitions, your faith. We need them! And when you arrive where we have not yet reached, have the patience to wait for us."[164]

*Given in Loreto, at the Shrine of the Holy House,*
*on March 25, Solemnity of the Annunciation*
*of the Lord, in the year 2019,*
*the seventh of my Pontificate.*

*Franciscus*

---

164 *Prayer Vigil with Young Italians at the Circus Maximus in Rome* (August 11, 2018): *L'Osservatore Romano*, August 13-14, 2018, 6.